YOU
inc.

YOU inc.

How to attract amazing success into your life and business

John McGrath

HarperCollins*Publishers*

HarperCollins*Publishers*

First published in Australia in 2003
by HarperCollins*Publishers* Pty Limited
A member of the HarperCollinsPublishers (Australia) Pty Limited Group

Copyright © John McGrath 2003

The right of John McGrath to be identified as the moral rights author of this work has been asserted by him in accordance with the
Copyright Amendment (Moral Rights) Act 2000 (Cth).

HarperCollins*Publishers*
25 Ryde Road, Pymble, Sydney NSW 2073, Australia
31 View Road, Glenfield, Auckland 10, New Zealand
77–85 Fulham Palace Road, London W6 8JB, United Kingdom
2 Bloor Street East, 20th floor, Toronto, Ontario M4W 1A8, Canada
10 East 53rd Street, New York NY 10022, USA

National Library of Australia Cataloguing-in-Publication data:

McGrath, John, 1963– .
    You inc.: how to attract amazing success into your life.
    ISBN 0 7322 7636 5.
    1. Success in business. 2. Success. I. Title.
658.4

Produced by Brewster Publishers Pty Ltd
Cover design by Cameron Hearne with Young & Rubicam, Sydney
Internal design by Brewster Publishers Pty Ltd
Printed and bound in Australia by Griffin Press on 79gsm Bulky Paperback White

10 9   05 06 07

Contents

Acknowledgements

Whilst my name sits proudly on the cover of this book, the names of so many other people deserve to sit beside it, as I am really just a product of my relationships, experiences and observations.

I have been supported, inspired and guided by so many words of wisdom and I have been gifted to have such incredible friends, mentors and coaches in my life. And life, just like business, is very much a team sport. Nothing significant happens without the help, support and encouragement of many people over a long period of time. I would like to thank just a few who have been instrumental in my achievements.

Firstly to Pam Brewster, who believed enough in my story to encourage me to write this book. Michael O'Brien, Richard Lee and Michael Tsagaris, my first ever bosses, for being tough on me and teaching me that doing it the right way was the only way. Anthony Bell, my accountant and good friend, for his care and commitment to helping us keep getting better. Terri Sissian for being the best sounding board and gatekeeper ever, keeping the pressure on and being a wonderful friend. Grant Vandenburg for continuing to push me beyond my comfort zone and helping me laugh at life along the way. Brett Blundy for showing us all what can be done when you have a dream and are prepared to take action. Mike Sheargold for being the greatest business coach on the planet. Wendy McCarthy for telling it as it is (and always being right). Matt McGrath, the most gifted advertising mind in the country, but more importantly a great friend and brother. And finally, my incredible team at work. You guys inspire me every day and make working for our company the exciting adventure it is.

Introduction

Do you think this book can change your life?

I'm not fishing for compliments, I'm just curious about your expectations about what you can get out of this book. I believe your expectations have a lot to do with the outcomes you achieve in life. Whenever I read a book or attend a seminar I expect that I'll pick up at least one piece of information or strategy that will improve my life. And inevitably I do.

By staying aware and expecting something useful to emerge you'd be surprised how often it does. The movie *Sliding Doors* was a great metaphor for how your life can change dramatically at any given moment depending on how you respond to information you receive. So I hope as you read this book you'll have a mindset that's always on the look-out for your next *Sliding Door*... your next lifechanging piece of information.

It's an exciting time for businesspeople. There have never been so many opportunities in the world of business as there are today. We can all achieve more than ever before and in a much shorter timeframe than we previously could have ever imagined. This book is designed to be a catalyst for you to create the business of your dreams. No matter where you are now, it's possible to shift your business to a whole new level — to create a world-class business.

I have written the book just as I would say it. As if we were sitting down together to chat about my observations and experiences in business and life over a fresh cup of coffee. It's not meant to be highly polished and it's certainly not been sugar-coated. I've told it as I've experienced it. In fact, virtually every page is a reflection of my daily thoughts and actions as I run our exciting business.

I have divided the book into four sections. The first section outlines the self-beliefs, habits and attitudes you need to cultivate as your foundation for success in business. The second section discusses the nitty-gritty of business operations. In section three you'll learn how to create a world-class business culture and lead your team. The final section covers sales and marketing and has my best advice on how to become a better salesperson.

I have included many 'take-a-ways' in the book, little things that you can implement in your business right away, as well as some major concepts and key lessons that will help you achieve success in the long run. It's a matter of grasping the basic ideas, putting them into action, and then gathering momentum.

I hope you take what I offer and use it in your own way. Everyone is different. Whilst there are some universal principals and common denominators that have evolved over time, you can create a successful business with your own personality and in your own style.

I have prepared this collection of tactics, strategies and insights in the hope that you will look at it often. As you read each page ask yourself, 'How can I apply this to my life right now?' and then take action. Greatness is not inherited by a select few. It is available to every one of us and is learned and applied one step at a time. So design your ideal business and your ideal life and make them masterpieces in progress.

You Inc.: Your Own Professional services company

It doesn't matter what stage of your career you're at or what your official job title is, you can start building your marketing and business skills right now. All it takes is a new mindset. From now on, consider yourself as your own professional services company: You Inc. It doesn't matter whether you're a driveway attendant at a petrol station or you're a brand marketing manager, you're a business.

I look forward to finding out how you enjoy this book and the greatest gift I could ask for would be for you to put some of these ideas to work in your business. To do something today as a result of an idea you pick up on these pages.

Carpe diem.

PART ONE

You+

1.

Anyone can succeed

Do you sincerely want to succeed? Do you deserve to succeed? Do you believe you can succeed? These are crucial questions to ask yourself, because unless you can answer them all with a resounding 'yes', chances are you won't succeed.

Undoubtedly the biggest obstacle to achieving success is your own negative self-belief. Whether you believe you can or you believe you can't, you're probably right. So to get you started on your way to success I've given you some useful tools for transforming your beliefs and expectations into a solid foundation for success. But first, let's work out your definition of what success is.

What is success for you?

'There is only one success — to be able to spend your life in your own way.'
CHRISTOPHER MORLEY

Before you set out to be successful you've got to decide what success is for you. It's no good wanting to have Richard Branson's success, or your parents' success or your friends' success, because we're all individuals with our own needs and values and our own definitions of success.

So take a minute to think about your personal definition of success. Because it's pretty hard to get up every morning and get fired up if you don't know what you're aiming at.

For me, success is about finding satisfaction in a number of different areas of my life. Firstly there's health. I like to keep fit and healthy, because I think without health you have nothing. Then there are my relationships. Having nourishing relationships with my partner, family and friends is one of life's greatest gifts. Also, if I can say I've surrounded myself with some of the most incredible people on the planet, and I enjoy their company on a regular basis, that's success to me.

Then there's personal development, which is important to me. I think human beings are learning beings — we're here to learn and grow. I'm a committed lifetime learner — that's a major part of my journey. I also value my spiritual development. Not in a religious sense so much, but simply developing love, compassion and care for my fellow human beings.

Contribution is part of my definition of success — making a contribution to my community and the world. That can be anything from giving a speech to the fifth class at Glenmore Road Public School to building a business that provides a career and lifestyle for hundreds of people and enables them to support their families.

And finally there's financial success. For me, that's about having financial freedom, not just more money. I don't think someone who has $10 million is necessarily more successful than someone who has $1 million. But I think it's important to get to a point of financial security in your life, so you're not constantly worrying about finding next month's rent.

Adjust your success thermostat

You're probably familiar with thermostats found in central heating and air-conditioning units. You set your desired room temperature and the thermostat maintains it while the temperature outside rises or falls.

You might not be aware of it, but each of us has an in-built success thermostat. It relates to your expectations of what level of success you can achieve. Because most people aren't aware they have a success thermostat they haven't realised they can adjust the setting. Many of us just leave it on the default setting, which is usually determined by the expectations we picked up from our early environment and peer group.

But it's important to realise that you can adjust your success thermostat to any level you desire.

What is your success thermostat set at right now? To find out, think about the key areas of your life: your relationships, health, personal development, career and finances. What do you expect for yourself in these areas? Do you expect to have deep, rich relationships with those you love? Do you believe you can have excellent health and live until you're 100? Do you understand that you can be independently wealthy and free of financial pressures within five years, no matter what your current financial situation is?

Your answers to these questions indicate what level your success thermostat is set to. If it's on a low setting, when an opportunity arises, your thermostat kicks in and you will self-sabotage and not reap the maximum benefit from the situation.

I've seen countless talented salespeople handicapped like this. They have an incredible start to their selling month, perhaps reaching their sales targets in the first week.

But this doesn't fit in with their expectations, so their success thermostat kicks in with a barrage of self-doubt. 'It must have been a fluke to start the month so well...I'll probably start struggling or hit the wall soon...I bet some of my current orders will cancel...' and so on.

The point I'm making is that you can only achieve up to the level of your expectations. So if you want better results you've got to adjust your success thermostat to boiling point by significantly raising your expectations.

If you're good enough, you're old enough

Some people think they're too old to succeed in business. Some think they're too young. Either way, it will become your reality if that's what you choose to believe. It's more productive to look for examples of people who succeeded in business at a very young or advanced age. Colonel Sanders developed his recipe for Kentucky Fried Chicken (or KFC as it's now known) when he was 65. Bill Gates went into business assembling and selling computers on his college campus when he was 20. Age is irrelevant unless you make it relevant.

Possible for you, possible for me

My business coach Michael Sheargold told me long ago that whatever success had been achieved by anyone else in the world of business was available to me too. Wow! 'So great empires that have been built, fortunes that have been made, sales records that have been set can all be achieved by any of us?' I asked.

'Exactly,' he replied. Michael then told me one of his favourite sayings is: 'If it's possible for you then it's possible for me, it's just a matter of how.'

That thought often enters my head when I'm disappointed with the results I'm getting. I keep remembering if someone else can do it, so can I. I just have to find the right approach.

So the next time you hear about someone doing something that really excites you, something that you'd love to do yourself, don't think, 'I wonder how on earth that was possible?' Ask yourself a better question: 'What would I have to do or change to make that happen for me?'

That's exactly how I grew my business. My aim was to build one of the best real estate companies in the world. So I researched who were the current market leaders, not just locally but anywhere in the world. Then I travelled to see these companies, met the people running them, and observed them in action.

I then refined many of these concepts and adapted them for my company. At no stage did I ever doubt I could create a world-class business. Uncertainty never entered my mind. The only thing I focused on was 'How can I improve what's been done, and when can I start?'

Improve your outcomes

Here are five tips to help you improve your outcomes:
1. Study the success of others
2. Eliminate the clutter and frenzy from your life
3. Find something to improve on every day
4. Embrace change with a positive attitude
5. Monitor and analyse your activities and outcomes weekly

Why do some people struggle in a world of abundance?

In life and in business it's important to have an abundance mentality. An abundance mentality says every business on the planet can thrive. The success of one business doesn't mean others must suffer.

And yet many businesses are struggling. My guess is that 80% of businesspeople are struggling to some extent. They're either coasting in their comfort zone, worried about the present and the future, or possibly about to go under.

If we asked them why their businesses weren't performing as well as they'd like, I'm sure they'd have plenty of reasons. Interest rates are too high, competitors are cutting their prices, the economy, etc, etc. These are genuine challenges to business, but some businesses still manage to thrive despite these conditions.

I believe the most fundamental things that determine success or failure in business are the beliefs and attitudes of the business leaders. Your beliefs create your reality, so forming positive beliefs is the first step towards achieving positive outcomes.

Having an abundance mentality — which is just something I have chosen to believe in — allows me to see opportunities that are hidden in less than ideal circumstances, and as a result, make the most out of any situation.

The fact that 90% of businesses fail in the first five years might be off-putting to someone starting out. But if it were me, I'd immediately focus on the 10% of businesses that do succeed. What models, methods and philosophies did these businesses use that allowed them to flourish? I'd identify these factors and replicate them in my own business.

If your business needs to grow, you need to grow. As obvious as this may sound, there are few people who approach business with this attitude. You have to drop your excuses and take a look at how you have created the situation you're in. Not many people are willing to hold themselves responsible for their business's lacklustre performance.

But if you can accept responsibility, and realise the adjustments you need to make to your beliefs and attitudes, you gain the power to make changes for the better.

Look for the factors that can provide impetus and support your endeavours. One of my guiding principles is that every situation, good or bad, offers a gift that provides some benefit. It's just a matter of finding the gift. Many people are overtaken by events, quick to declare them a setback or disaster. Instead, you can ask, 'Where's the gift in this?'

Life happens, and in business there will always be changes and challenges to the status quo. New businesses opening, competitors cutting costs, staff defecting to the opposition, changes in legislation. Just keep your focus on what you can control. Avoid diluting your energy on issues that may be relatively trivial in the long run.

When I started out in 1989 I was surrounded by people telling me, 'The market is collapsing — you're crazy to start a business now.' But I chose not to dwell on the falling market, high interest rates and the critics. Instead I placed my focus on what actions were necessary to create a world-class business. I rose every morning with the thoughts, 'What do I have to do? Who do I have to recruit? How should I answer the phone? How should we treat our customers?'

Building positive self belief

Your beliefs create your reality. It's like Henry Ford once said: 'If you think you can or think you can't, you're right.' Some people have a tendency towards doubt and negative self beliefs, which can really hold them back. If you fall into this category the good news is that you can change and be more positive about yourself by making an effort to change your thinking.

Catch yourself saying things that are negative, sceptical or cynical, and one by one eradicate them from your inner and outer dialogue. Choose to focus on all the positives and the things that are going right in your life, rather than the things that aren't going right. Seek inspiration in stories of people who have done great things. Reading about people who have achieved great results shows you what's possible and gives you a blast of positive energy.

One of the ways I have changed my beliefs is by constantly looking for people who are doing it better. Not just in my industry, but anywhere.

Fast growth is a natural state

If you have come to the conclusion that you've been under-performing in the game of life and the world of business, you might be wondering how long it will take you to improve your situation. It's my belief that people can turn themselves around a lot quicker than they think. And not only is rapid change possible, it's also very beneficial to everyone involved.

Long, arduous processes of change rarely work. People get bored and drift back into their old habits. People who are taking an eternity to change key areas of their lives are out of touch with today's world. They don't realise that a paradigm shift in their attitudes can bring quick results.

Want to lose weight the healthy way? Six weeks can get most people pretty close to their ideal outcome (unless you've been really bad!). Want to move up the corporate ladder? Give it 12 months. How about massively increasing your sales? About 90 days.

I'm not suggesting the initial move from where you are to your ideal outcome will be easy. But I guarantee you can change virtually anything that's not working in your life within months, not years, if you develop an effective set of beliefs, expectations and actions and are committed to achieving results.

Fast growth also benefits everyone, not just you. Think about it. As your business grows, consider the number of people that benefit. First, you. You develop more skills, earn more money and build your self-esteem.

Secondly, your employees. They're involved in the exciting buzz that surrounds a company on the move. They can climb the ladder and build their roles within your growth. They can usually earn more money as the demands and needs of a growing business reward those that step up to the plate.

Thirdly, your customers benefit, as you usually only achieve growth by offering superior service, providing superior quality or more cost-effective products.

Nine strategies to move ahead fast

1. Be totally clear about what you want.
2. Know that anything is possible.
3. Surround yourself with great people and BIG thinkers.
4. Always do what you promise to do.
5. Set high standards for yourself and others and don't accept anything less.
6. Focus on what matters and what you can control.
7. Put in place systems that deliver every time.
8. Take action now – momentum leads to greatness.
9. Keep doing whatever it takes until you achieve your outcome.

Fourthly, the community. The more your business grows the more jobs you can offer, the more taxes you'll contribute to the community, the more community events you'll be able to support. A business that's static is actually losing all of these natural benefits of growth.

The Bears murdered the Swans

A few years ago I attended a football match between the Sydney Swans and the Brisbane Bears. Both teams were in great form and near the top of the ladder. It was expected to be one of the best matches of the season.

The game was divided into four 30-minute quarters. At the end of the first quarter the Swans, whom I support, had taken control and were leading by two goals. By half-time the Swans had a strong six-goal lead. I couldn't wait to see them finish off the Bears.

But something happened in that 10-minute break between halves. There were no injuries. The weather didn't change. Who knows what went through the minds of the players in the dressing room. But two very different teams took the field for the third-quarter.

After 15 minutes the scores were level. By the end of the quarter the Bears had taken control. They extended their lead in the last quarter to be the convincing winners on the day.

So, what happened? Within minutes the game had flipped 180 degrees. The team that had dominated the game for the entire first half was licking its wounds. And the team that looked like it was finished by half-time was celebrating its huge win.

What happened in the half-time break is what often happens to many businesses and salespeople. The things that had created success were lost. The focus and determination of the first half became self-doubt and uncertainty. The Swans started wondering if they could hold on, while the Bears developed a laser beam focus on winning the game at any cost. The teams were physically unchanged but mentally the Bears had won the battle.

The greatest competitor you'll ever come up against is self-doubt

Thinking you might not achieve your goals or you're not worthy of success — these thoughts will inevitably lead to failure unless you can arrest them and turn them around. Again, awareness of your state of mind and clarity about your goals has a major impact on your outcomes. When the self-doubting dialogue enters your head, choose whether to accept it, reject it or use it to your benefit.

So in the dressing room at half-time what could the Swans' coach have asked his players? 'What do we need to do to ensure we win this game?' That's a better quality question to be pondering than, 'Oh God, I wonder if we can keep the lead?'

He could have asked the players, 'What would have to happen now to take us from a 12-point advantage to a 32-point advantage in the next 30 minutes?' Because you can guarantee the team were thinking, 'The opposition is going to come out firing, I wonder if we can hang on?' That question has a very different outcome to 'What do we have to do to double the size of our lead?'

Ask better questions

Whether you're winning or losing in a situation the process is the same: ask quality questions. The same situation occurs in business. People say, 'I wonder how long we can hang on?' But it all comes back to the clarity of your thinking and the quality of the questions you're asking yourself.

If my sales team says the market is hard, I say go harder. You adapt to the circumstances, and whether you're the leader or the challenger in a situation you can still always ask better questions. It's an ever-changing dialogue, but in the end the result comes down to the quality of questions you're asking.

The concept here is: the better quality questions you ask yourself, the better quality answers you have. The better quality answers you have, the better quality outcomes you're going to achieve.

2.

Establishing what you want to achieve

Before Michelangelo sculpted his superb statue of David it was just a slab of shapeless, rough marble. But Michelangelo saw beyond the rough exterior. He had a vision of a great masterpiece and he chipped away at the marble, one piece at a time, one day at a time, until he had realised his vision.

Like Michelangelo's marble, all of us start out as a huge bundle of potential. To create a masterpiece of your life you must see the opportunity that lies beneath your current reality. Developing a clear vision of the life you want to lead is the first step on the road to success.

What do you really want?

Before you read any further I want to make sure you get exactly what you need out of this book... and the only way that will happen is if you're absolutely clear about what you really want.

When you finish reading this book, what would be an ideal outcome? What would you seek to get more clarity on? What skills would you like to hone? What areas of your life do you need to get inspired about?

If you have 100% clarity about what's important in your life, half the battle is won. You need to know what needs to be improved, and what needs to be eradicated. The next critical step is to make a move in the direction of the changes and outcomes you want to see. Once you've pushed through the inertia and gained some of the momentum you need, it starts to become easier.

So take a minute right now and jot down the five things that you are committed to getting out of this book. The order is unimportant, and you can alter the list later, but it's important at this minute to write down the list.

Repack your bags

Recently I was in San Diego at a business conference. On the second day I attended a workshop called Repack Your Bags, by Richard Leider. I knew nothing about the session but was intrigued by the session name, so I decided to check it out.

I walked into the room and there were about twenty people there. A small bearded man with a flipchart and marker pen stood up the front. On a piece of butcher's paper he had written 'Repack Your Bags'.

I was a bit alarmed at the contrast from the other sessions I'd attended. They were held in the main conference room, with its beautiful stage and three huge projector screens for their slick PowerPoint presentations. Yet Leider had opted for a small room, tucked away in a corner of the hotel, and a few simple sheets of butcher's paper.

I only had a few moments to decide whether to stay, or find another workshop. But before I had made up my mind Leider saw me, smiled and said, 'Please come in and join us — there's a seat up here in the front row.' Now I was obliged to stay and listen. From my front row seat a discreet escape would be impossible.

I felt irritation at having my options whipped away from me, but then I decided to change my attitude and look for the lesson.

Leider handed us some notes titled 'The Good Life Inventory'. Consistent with his overall presentation they were rough around the edges — a few photocopied sheets stapled together.

I looked at the first question: 'Are you living in the place where you belong, with the people you love, doing the right work, on purpose?'

Wow! It made me think. In fact, it made me damned uncomfortable. (For me this is a good state to be in.) Discomfort or frustration usually motivates me to take swift and immediate action to improve my situation.

He discussed how life is made up of different cycles. There are plateaus — times when you reach a comfort zone and settle into a lifestyle, career or social group. Few changes occur during these phases.

And then there are catalysts or triggers as he called them: situations or events that cause you to reassess your life. They challenge you, inspire you and inform you. These times can be pleasant or very uncomfortable. They include such things as marriage, divorce, starting a business, being financially challenged, taking an overseas trip, someone taking advantage of you and being inspired by a seminar or a great book.

Whatever the trigger may be, it gives you the opportunity to change. It may even force you to change what you're doing or rethink the next phase of your life. To repack your bags.

While I'd had plenty of catalysts in my life, I'd never really thought of allowing those times to prompt me to repack my bags. To review the way I did things, abandon old habits, and perhaps pick up some new skills or attitudes that would better equip me for the immediate road ahead.

Suddenly it seemed obvious that I needed to constantly re-evaluate the contents of my bag (read my habits). Are the things I've packed useful — are they appropriate for the journey that lies ahead?

Are your current skills, habits and actions what you need to achieve the goals you've set for yourself? Do you need to adjust or refine your methods, time management or workspace? Do you have the right support team around you to achieve big goals? Is there anything you need to leave behind to clear the path to your next destination?

Take a moment to capture and consider the things that came to mind as you read these paragraphs. What are you lacking? Where are you overcommitted? What distractions do you need to deal with to allow you to travel lighter, to travel faster?

Dump the tomorrow fantasy - if it ain't happening now it probably won't

Some people talk a lot of 'gonna'. You know, they say, 'One day I'm gonna do this', or 'Next year I'm gonna do that'. The reality is, if you're not doing it now, you're probably not going to do it. So do it now - start with a small step today.

If you've been thinking about improving your relationship, go home tonight and tell your partner how much you appreciate them. If you've been saying 'I'm going on a diet' for a year, start your diet at lunchtime by ordering a salad sandwich instead of a burger. If you've been promising yourself to ramp-up your business for the past five years, sit down today and draw up a list of actions and get started today, before you go home.

And if you're not prepared to make some changes, it's better just to accept things as they are now and be honest with yourself, rather than waste your energy on a tomorrow fantasy.

Goal setting

'The greatest danger for most of us is not that our aim is too high and we miss it, but that it is too low and we reach it.' MICHELANGELO

A lot of people have lost the sense of excitement about their lives. Not only about the next twelve months, but also about the next twelve years. 'Last year wasn't that great. Why would next year be any different?' they think.

This is where you have to change your energy. You've got to say, 'Maybe the last twelve months weren't so great, but the next twelve months can be the best of my life.' And the way to have a great year is to set some goals that you can get excited about and then take the necessary action to make them happen.

So let's dream for a minute. Let's imagine you could set aside your fear of failure and achieve any goal you wanted with 100% certainty. What goals would really juice you up and get you excited?

You might say, 'Maybe if I pay off my credit card bill...' Good start. But why not take it to the next level. What if you paid the card off, and had $10,000 in the bank? 'Well, that would be great', you say.

Now we're on a roll: no debt, $10,000 in the bank... what about a dream holiday? 'I'd love to go to Italy, but it'll never happen.' Let's write it down anyway. Let's say in twelve months' time you've paid off your credit card, saved $10,000, booked a holiday to Italy, bought a new car, got a promotion and your income has doubled. How would that feel? 'Well... fantastic!' OK, let's make it happen.

We'll start with the debt. We need to find a way for you to save about $300 per week. 'But I don't earn enough', you say. So you're in sales — what would it take to double your income? 'I'd have to double my sales.' OK, you need to spend an extra hour a day prospecting. Let's do it. Write it in your diary.

So you see, this is a process to achieve success. Dream about where you would like your life to be, translate those dreams into goals, and then work out the actions required to achieve the goals. Everyone can break down their dreams into bite-size chunks — phone calls, meetings, appointments, and emails: that's all it takes.

Visualise your success

Ask yourself these questions: What would I do right now if I knew I couldn't fail? How would I be planning my life? What steps would I be taking? These are important questions, because people who succeed in business think like this. They almost always start from nothing and have to visualise and internalise their success before it materialises. As bestselling self-help author Wayne Dyer says, 'You'll see it when you believe it.'

Daring to dream

When I was 18 I totally immersed myself in self-education and personal development. I came across some motivational tapes by Zig Ziglar and really loved them. So when I heard he was coming to Sydney to give a two-day seminar I just knew I had to be there, even though the ticket cost me more than a week's pay.

I was so keen I got a seat in the middle of the front row and was hanging off his every word. At the end of the first day Ziglar said, 'OK, who in this room believes that setting goals is important?' Everybody put their hand up. Then he said, 'Excellent. So, who in the room has written goals that they can stand up and show me now?'

Only six people out of the 200 in the room put their hands up. I wasn't one of them. 'We have a disconnect here,' Ziglar said, 'all of you agree that goals are necessary, but only three per cent of you have them written down.' So he set us some homework. He told us not to come back tomorrow unless we'd written out our goals. 'We'll refund your money if you like,' he said, 'but don't come back if you haven't got a list of your goals.'

So I went home and started writing out my goals. It was hard work getting my first few goals down on paper. I was afraid to dream about how my life could be and felt a little embarrassed. My inner critic was saying, 'Nah, that's not going to happen.' But I stuck with it and all of a sudden it started flowing.

I started thinking I'd like to have some money in the bank, so I wrote that down. Then I thought it would be good to have a nice car, so I wrote that down. And wouldn't it be good to travel around the world one day? So I wrote that down, and on it went. Before long I had four or five pages.

By writing down those goals and daring to dream about how I wanted my life to be — how my life *could* be — I opened up a whole new world of possibilities. I went to the second day of the seminar a changed person.

I was back in the front row again at 9 a.m. and Ziglar asked, 'Now you've got your list of goals, what are you going to do with it? Put them in your top drawer?' Someone put their hand up and said, 'No, you've got to look at it regularly.' Ziglar asked how often we should look at our list of goals. 'Maybe once a month to check if you're on track,' somebody suggested.

'That's a great start,' Ziglar replied, 'but how about every day?' Just as I was wondering how I was going to get the discipline to look at my list of goals every day, he said, 'or maybe twice a day — first thing in the morning, and again before you go to bed?'

So I undertook to do that. Every day since that seminar 20 years ago, I've looked at my goals twice a day. I knew that to make it work I had to make it easy to do. So I laminated my list of goals and stuck it to my shower wall. It's still there today (although I've changed the list dozens of times), and I review it every time I take a shower.

This one simple action has brought more results and more positive changes into my life than any other activity since then.

Shower power

Twice a day I go over my success questions and daily affirmations:

Success questions

- Why am I blessed and fortunate to be alive today? What are the things in my life that make me happy?
- What will I do to make a difference in someone's life today?
- Who do I love in my life? Why do I love them? How will I show them today?
- What will I do to surprise my partner and friends and make them smile?
- Who can I catch doing something right today? Who can I show compassion to and support during challenging times?
- How will I convert a current Customer to a Raving Fan today? What will I do today to increase my business tomorrow?
- How will I exercise today to increase my energy and make me stronger?
- What fruit will I eat this morning to give me quick energy and cleanse me?
- What book will I read or tape will I listen to, to enlighten and inspire me?
- Will today's activities keep me on track to live my dreams? What seed will I plant for future growth?

Daily affirmations

- Today I'm going to be magnificent! I love the adventure of each day.
- I am in charge of my happiness; nobody can take away the magic of this day.
- I power through my day with focus, energy and enthusiasm and achieve goals with ease.
- Everything in life serves me as a reward or lesson.
- I only focus on what matters and let other issues pass me by.
- I always encourage others. I am compassionate and supportive.
- I contribute to and support the underprivileged, the community, and I care for the environment.
- I have everything I need right now to accomplish everything I want. I live my life with balance and harmony.

Running out of the fog

A lot of people spend their lives running in the fog. They keep busy, going from one appointment to the next, dealing with issues as they arise. At the end of the day they slouch in their lounge chairs in front of the TV and have a beer or a glass of wine and zone out until the next day when they do it all again. They're not really conscious of where they are or where they're going. They just put one foot in front of the other.

Goal setting is a way to get your head out of the fog. It takes you away from the day to day issues that surround you, and gives you some clarity about the life you'd really like to be living.

A couple of days after Zig Ziglar's seminar I was working on my goals in my lunch hour. I had fifteen minutes before I had to be back at work. I was sitting in the sun on a milk crate in Stanley

Street, Darlinghurst thinking about my life. I was 18 years old, just bombed out of school, a trainee car salesman, in debt and with a minuscule wage.

It was really hard for me to think about having a better life, because up until then I'd been so busy worrying about all my problems and what wasn't going right in my life. But as I started working on my goals and focusing on where I wanted to go, my attitude totally changed. All my present difficulties seemed insignificant. I saw them as minor setbacks on the way to where I was going.

I maintained that attitude through the tough times when I was starting my business. I set myself some pretty big goals. I wanted to have the best real estate company on the planet, but it was hard in the early days to really believe I could achieve that.

Reviewing your goals

If you're going over your goals daily it will soon become obvious if you're not making progress towards one or more of them. If this is the case, then it's time to review those goals. If a goal is no longer compelling, it's best to drop it off your list. I'm a great believer in less is more. It's better to have 10 compelling goals that really fire you up, than 25 goals that are only of some interest to you.

If a goal is still compelling but you're not making progress towards it, then review your action plan and see what additional steps you could take to achieve it. Ask yourself what's been holding you back. Is it a belief pattern? Is it a resource that you need to bring into your life? Maybe you need to reprioritise it.

But I stuck with my goals and worked through the obstacles. Slowly things started to happen. I started to make some progress and had a few small wins. With every small step forward my belief that I could achieve my goals strengthened.

3.

Understanding what it will take to get there

Once you've established what you want to achieve you're ready to start working towards your goals. Achieving success is largely about changing to new habits. Personal development coach Brian Tracey defined success as a few simple disciplines repeated daily over an extended period. Similarly, failure is a few errors in judgment repeated daily over an extended period.

Your old habits are deeply embedded because of the time you've spent repeating them. To change your habits it's helpful to have a look at the self-beliefs that are underpinning them. We often develop a myriad of negative beliefs, low expectations, fears and doubts that get in the way of our success. Success is not really possible until you believe it's possible for you. The good news is you can change your negative self-beliefs in an instant.

Changing in the moment

All sorts of things happen in life that you have no control over. Some good, some bad. You can't stop the bad things happening to you. But what you can control is how you react to them. You've planned a picnic for the weekend and spent all Saturday preparing the food. When you wake up on Sunday, it's pouring with rain. A disaster or a minor inconvenience? That all depends on your attitude.

If you're in disaster mode you get upset, curse the weather, and lament all the effort you've wasted. Alternatively you could be thrilled you've got a whole week's worth of great lunches to take to work and then head out to the cinema with a friend to catch a movie you've wanted to see. You can't stop the rain, but you can change your attitude.

At any given moment in your life, you choose the mood you're in. And you can go from feeling stress and panic to being calm and positive in an instant. You can change in the moment.

Freeze-frame

Recently a friend of mine, Maggie Webber, demonstrated changing in the moment at a seminar for our sales team. She got one of our team members at the front of the room and hooked him up to a heart monitor so everyone could see his pulse rate. Then she got him to do some stressful activities such as singing a song in front of the group. As he became stressed we could watch his heart rate soar.

Then Maggie asked him to visualise a pleasant scenario. She got him thinking about his favourite holiday destination and people he'd like to spend time with there. After some pleasant thoughts of sitting on the porch of a lovely weekender, chatting and joking with a favourite friend, his pulse rate quickly dropped. In a moment he'd gone from being stressed out to a calm, pleasant space.

Maggie does what she calls 'freeze-frame', or 'changing in the moment', which you can use whenever you're feeling stressed. In the midst of all your turbulent thoughts, just stop, take a deep breath and say to yourself, 'I need to change my dialogue. I will get through this; it will not destroy me. This will make me stronger.'

Ask yourself what's the gift in this situation? What's the best emotion for me to hold around this right now? What's the best thing for me to do right now? Because when your attitude changes your whole energy changes and you can massively change the outcome of an event.

You can change your business in three seconds

You can create a world-class business in just three seconds. That's the time it takes for you to decide that you will have a world-class business. Everything else is just implementation or execution.

So make that decision right now. There's absolutely nothing to stop you from deciding to pursue your ultimate goal right now (except possibly you).

When I started my real estate business I decided right at the outset that it would be a world-class business. While others were focused on keeping their heads above water, I was visualising something great: an organisation that would change the way real estate is bought and sold worldwide.

Once you've made the commitment it changes the way you look at things. If you're going to have a world-class business, what sort of people should you employ? Only the best, or those who are committed to becoming the best. What about your systems? Will they cope, or will they need to be redesigned to accommodate your increases in business?

How about the structure of your business? It may work now, but you'd better start looking into something that will work in a much bigger marketplace.

Every action you take is underpinned by your decision to be world class. Change your decisions and you change your actions. Change your actions and you change your results.

In the early days of my career I was selling houses at an average price of around $200,000. Not the bottom end of the market, but certainly in the lower quartile. One day I got a call from a friend who told me he knew someone who wanted to sell a $10 million property. Was I interested in selling it?

My reaction was, 'I can't.' My view of my sales ability was too limited, so I turned him down. After I hung up the phone I gave it some thought. Surely it couldn't be that much different from selling a $200,000 property... could it?

Right then and there I made the decision to sell that property. Nothing else had changed. My experience and knowledge remained exactly the same. But I had made a mental shift from 'I can't' to 'Why not?'

I rang my friend back and told him that I'd never sold a property of that value, but I'd like to discuss it with the owner. A meeting was arranged. Needless to say the client had never heard of my company and seemed to be giving me time out of courtesy to his friend who had recommended me. We spoke for about an hour and I made a commitment to return with a sales strategy. He was seeing three other agents that day.

The next 24 hours changed my life. I wasn't just hoping I'd get this piece of business — every cell of my body was committed to it. On sheer adrenalin I produced the best sales strategy I'd ever written. I didn't get it back to him the next day. I got it back to him that night. I sat with him and explained my thoughts and strategy. I left the house at about 10 p.m. He decided during that meeting to let me look after his sale.

Take stock for a minute. How many times have you been presented with a wonderful opportunity, then pulled back, rejecting or not pursuing potential business because of your limiting beliefs and low expectations?

If, in that brief moment following the phone call from my friend, I hadn't changed my beliefs from impossible to possible, my future could have been very different.

The story ended well. We sold his house for $11.25 million, an Australian record at the time. My mindset was changed, we generated amazing publicity for the company, and entered a new realm of the market. And no, it wasn't any different to selling a $200,000 property; there were just a few more zeros on the commission cheque.

If nothing changes, nothing changes

Sounds obvious, doesn't it? But how many people in business expect things to get better without being committed to making the necessary changes?

The waiting game rarely provides what you want. Hoping your sales will increase without an intelligent, simple plan backed up by steely determination is naïve. Recognise that for things to change, you have to be the driver of change. You have to reinvent yourself.

The only thing in the world that you truly control is yourself. You can't control your customers, competitors, economic conditions or your business partners. But you can control you. Each decision you make, each action you take, is 100% controllable and up to you.

As you read this book keep thinking about you. What do I have to do today to effect the change I want in the world? That may be a scary concept because you might have become accustomed to blaming everything and everyone else for your situation. The realisation that you've created your outcomes, and only you can change the situation for the better, can be very daunting.

If that sounds like you, get over it and wake up to the truth of life: you create your whole reality.

The situation you're in right now is the result of all your beliefs and actions up until today. And more importantly, your future world is dependent upon the decisions and actions you take from this moment forward.

So if you want better results in life you have to work out what changes you need to make, and then make them.

I'll give you an example. I gave Robert, one of my salespeople, a lead on someone who was interested in selling their property. I said, 'Give him a call. I've dealt with him before and I know he wants to sell.'

I spoke to Robert the next morning and asked how he went. He told me they'd spoken and had arranged to meet on Thursday. I asked him, 'If you arrive on time on Thursday and do everything right, you've got a chance of getting his business'. He agreed.

'But imagine if you drove past his property last night — it's on your way home — and you called him from outside and said to him: 'Mr Smith, I wanted to let you know that I've just driven past your place and I'm really looking forward to meeting with you on Thursday. I couldn't wait to tell you I've already thought of three or four potential buyers I'm currently working with, who I think would be very interested. I'm going to bring a printout from our database about these people. I'm really excited about the meeting, and thanks for the opportunity.'

'So when you arrive on Thursday you're going to have a much better chance of getting the business. Your chance of success will probably have risen 100% based on one quick phone call.'

Robert took that tip on board and has adopted it as part of his communication plan. He tells me, 'John, when I arrive they treat me like a member of the family. They're excited to see me rather than being scared.'

So by taking a small piece of advice and being willing to change his sales routine, Robert was able to improve his results.

Imagine how well you could perform if you picked up a new piece of information every day, absorbed it and implemented it. It would have a tremendous effect on your life as you change your actions each day.

Competence happens in a moment

Imagine a six-year-old child who's just got a bike for Christmas. He gets on the bike and falls straight over. Gets back on the bike, wobbles a bit and falls over again. After about 17 attempts, he gets on the bike, goes five metres, starts wobbling, straightens up the handlebars and then rides on. In a single moment the child knew he could ride the bike. So what happened in that moment? Competence happened. He suddenly understood he could ride the bike, and off he went.

The same principle applies to businesspeople when they're learning new skills and adopting new behaviours. At first it might seem difficult. You don't think you can do it. You have some failures. It seems like it's not working. But if you just keep at it you'll soon see some small wins and one day competence will just happen.

I've seen it with salespeople. They come on board, they miss, they miss, they're doing poorly. They're under pressure, they're stressed. All of a sudden they have a small win, a bigger win, a bigger win, and BANG, all of a sudden they're great salespeople.

The importance of learning what holds you back

Imagine you're going sailing on Sydney Harbour. The sun is shining, there's a nice breeze blowing, the picnic lunch is packed, the drinks are chilled, the crew is ready and the yacht rigged up. Everything is perfect for a magnificent day on the water. But before you set out the first thing you have to do is untie the boat from the mooring. Because you're not going anywhere if the boat's still tied up.

Similarly, if you're going to have a magnificent life the first step is to untie the mooring lines that hold you back from success. Mooring lines are our limiting beliefs about ourselves and the world. Just as the yacht's mooring lines can't be seen below the water, we often don't see our mooring lines because they're subconscious.

The easiest way to identify your mooring lines is to take a few minutes to think about an area of your life where you'd like to perform better. Then finish this sentence: 'I'm not succeeding in this area of my life because...' Whatever comes out of your mouth after 'because' is probably a mooring line.

I'm always short of cash because... creative people never make any money.

I didn't get promoted because... there's a glass ceiling for women in my company.

My business is losing money because... the economy is bad.

I'm not getting ahead because... I'm from the wrong side of the tracks.

I'm not successful in my career because... I don't have enough education.

Now you've identified what your primary mooring lines are, it's time to release them. That means shifting your beliefs. And the best way to shift your beliefs is to find evidence to the contrary. Find examples that totally contradict your mooring lines.

If your mooring line is 'creative people never make any money', do some research on Russell Crowe, Bryce Courtenay, Kylie Minogue and other creative people who have made millions. If your mooring line is that a corporate glass ceiling exists for women, then look for examples of brilliant businesswomen that have gone to the top of the corporate ladder, such as Anita Roddick, who founded The Body Shop, Jillian Broadbent, who's on the Board of the Reserve Bank of Australia and a director of Coca-Cola Amatil Limited, or Julia Ross, one of Australia's few female self-made multi-millionaires.

We can always find some evidence to support our beliefs. If your mooring line is 'I can't get ahead because I'm from the wrong side of the tracks', you'll probably have some facts to back this up. 'None of my mates have been successful either.' What you need to do is look for some alternative facts that support a more empowering belief for you.

What if I was to tell you that over 80% of millionaires in America come from the wrong side of the tracks? What if you changed your *belief to being from the wrong side of the tracks is no impediment to success?* What's holding you back now?

The law of familiarity

If you become too familiar with something it's easy to lose your appreciation for it. It ceases to inspire and motivate you when you start taking it for granted. You might have a magnificent ocean view, but you walk by it every day and start to get blasé. One day a friend comes over and says, 'Wow! What an amazing view,' and you remember how lucky you are.

The same thing happens in business. Remember the day you started your job or your business. Remember how excited you were? Remember you were so proud you told everyone you knew? Are you still that excited and proud now? No? Well has something happened to diminish your excitement and pride, or has the law of familiarity kicked in?

The first customer enquiry I ever got for a sale property... I've got to tell you, I was so excited I was at their front door before they even put the phone down. And one thing that's helped me to become successful is that I've maintained that energy throughout my career. If someone rings up today and says, 'I want to sell my house', I'm just as excited to hear those words as I was 20 years ago.

What makes a difference – rate yourself from zero to ten

People can always find something to blame when their life's not working. The economy's flat, their partner doesn't understand them, competition is tough, there's a drought, there are no jobs for people with my experience, my boss doesn't like me, and so on.

Rarely do people consider that their problems have anything to do with them. They think their situation is always caused by external circumstances. Trouble is, you can't change external circumstances. So the only things that matter are things that you can control.

When I do live seminars I often get the audience thinking about what changes they could make to improve their lives. So if I'm talking to a room of insurance brokers I'll ask them to think about what the best insurance salesperson on the planet would be like. What would their strengths be? How would they look? How would they act? What habits would they have?

After some brainstorming we come up with a list of attributes: they'd be highly organised, have plenty of energy, they'd work hard, be good listeners, and have empathy, good communication skills and great product knowledge.

Then I'll ask the audience to rate themselves on each of these attributes from zero to 10, with 10 being the best, and zero the worst. If they're being completely honest the average rating is usually between five and seven for most of these skills.

So I ask them, 'Six out of 10 for organisation — will that help you get more customers?' The answer is no. 'Five out of 10 for hard work — is that going to sell more policies?' No. 'Seven out of 10 for communication — is that going to help you market your product?' Again, the answer is no.

The audience quickly realises that it's rarely external factors that created their situation. The real problem is they've allowed themselves, for whatever reason, to live life at 6 out of 10.

The good news is that the first step towards living a 10 out of 10 life is creating awareness that there's room for improvement. Just by doing this exercise you start to take control of your life and begin thinking about how to improve your ratings. So then I get them to make a plan. I get them to write down a few things that they could do to improve their ratings in key areas.

So now we've got awareness and a plan. What we need next is some motivation. To help get the audience motivated to make changes I ask them to think about how their lives would be if they were operating at an eight, nine or even a 10 in all these areas.

Rate yourself from zero to 10

1. Consider an aspect of your life that you want to improve. It could be relationships, career, finances, spirituality, anything at all.

2. Ask yourself what would someone who is currently outstanding in that area look like? What would their habits and qualities be? Write a list of attributes.

3. Rate yourself from zero to 10 on each attribute.

4. If you're below an 8, write a mini-plan to lift your rating.

5. Imagine yourself as a 9 or 10. How would your life be?

6. Stay focused on your outcomes as you make the changes.

As they imagine their ratings going up they see their sales increasing, their income goes up, their financial situation improves. With all these improvements they see their self esteem growing, their stress decreasing, and as a result, their relationships often get better. Everyone gets really excited.

Focusing on the positive outcomes of the changes gives you the impetus to actually make the changes. Because change always has a degree of pain in it, even if it's just overcoming the fear of the unknown. So by focusing on the rewards you can stick with your changes even if they feel a little bit uncomfortable at first.

Are you good enough to get better?

I'm sure you're already pretty good at what you do. And the fact that you're investing time in developing yourself by reading this book shows you're making an effort to get better. That's very important, because from my experience it's never about getting competent.

The real game is about becoming the very best you can be. And one of the challenges we face is continuing to learn once we've reached an acceptable level of competence.

Former UCLA basketball team coach John Wooden knew how to get the best out of his team. They won the National Collegiate Athletic Association championships 10 times — seven consecutively. This is one of the toughest sporting competitions in the world. His players were the Michael Jordans of tomorrow with huge talent and teenage egos.

Wooden could keep his players focused and grounded, and harness their enormous talent, year after year. At the start of each season Coach Wooden would gather his players and tell them how they could develop their skills to become the best players they could be.

He would start his address by saying, 'I want you to remember one thing — it's going to be what you learn after you know it all that will set you apart. So, are you good enough right now to get better?'

When I first heard this it hit me between the eyes. It was one of those many things I've heard during my life that stopped me in my tracks. I'd been seduced into thinking that you learn until you're competent or even very good at something, then you stop. This was a paradigm shift, thanks to Coach Wooden.

I listen to more inspirational tapes, go to more seminars, and read more books and business magazines than anyone I know on the planet. Some people say to me, 'Your business is going pretty well, why do you want to do that?' I reply, 'Because I want to know the next piece of information that's going to take me to the next level. I want to find out the next idea that I can pass on to my team and share with my managers. I want to get more motivated than I was yesterday and the day before.'

Accountability

Accountability is a great tool to ensure you move towards your goals. It's human nature not to want to let people down. So if you've made yourself accountable to someone you're much more likely to follow through on your intentions.

For example, if you're going to the gym at 6 a.m. on your own, you might be easily tempted to roll over and go back to sleep when the alarm goes off. But if you've arranged to meet a friend there, you're more likely to show, because you don't want to let them down.

I ensure I have accountability in my life by announcing my goals to my team. Whenever our internal strategy is revised, we tell the team. That makes it harder for us not to follow through on it. I meet monthly with my business coach. Our agenda is always to review the last 30 days. What were the goals we set for ourselves and how far did we go towards achieving them? What got in the way? What are the next goals? What's likely to get in the way? How can we deal with that?

If I have a public speaking engagement I'll take the opportunity to announce the initiatives we're undertaking and the directions in which we're heading. There are many opportunities to make yourself accountable. Tell your goals to your staff, your wife, your husband, your best friend or your mates at the pub. Just by making some form of verbal declaration of intention to anyone will increase your determination to follow through.

The importance of passion, energy and persistence

'Whenever anything is done, I have learned it is being done by a monomaniac with a mission.' PETER DRUCKER

You might think talent plays a big part in business success. Having a natural aptitude for business is certainly a great asset. But talent is a poor second to passion.

You see this a lot in sport. Often the most talented athletes have less motivation because they expect to win. If you get the jump on them they find it hard to bounce back. Their egos are large and get in the way. They fall prey to the less talented underdog with a burning passion to win.

It's the same in business. You need a fierce passion to succeed. There are lots of highly talented businesspeople who are unemployed or just surviving.

I'm just as excited about coming to work each day as I was twenty years ago. Seeing my team members develop their skills, seeing customers delighted — it means an enormous amount to me. My business is intimately connected to the essence of what I love about life. I get an enormous amount of satisfaction from it and that's how I maintain my enthusiasm for what I do.

People often ask me 'Don't you get tired? You seem to do so much in a day.' I tell them that's the secret. I truly believe that it's not the things you do in a day that make you tired, it's the things you leave undone or the opportunities you don't take.

Think about this scenario: It's 6:30 p.m. You've come home from work dog tired, feeling self-righteous, telling your partner how hard you've worked and how under-appreciated you are. The phone rings. It's Lotto calling to tell you that you've just won the carryover jackpot of $5 million, and you can pop in now to collect your cheque if you'd like to.

Still tired? I doubt it. You've snapped out of your fatigued state, leapt three feet in the air, grabbed your partner and done a quick waltz around the lounge room. You pick up your keys and head out the door with more energy than you've apparently had for years.

So were you really tired before you picked up the phone? Or were you just lacking something to get excited about? I think you know where I'm headed with this.

If you're lacking the energy for your work it's probably because it doesn't excite you any more. You need to rekindle your enthusiasm by getting your business more aligned with your passion. The best cure for fatigue is to have lots of projects that you're passionate and excited about.

Now that I've told you about passion and energy, I want to talk about persistence.

Persistence beats most other virtues. There will be plenty of challenges on the road to success. Your determination, self-beliefs and faith will be tested over and over.

Our company hasn't walked a path of gold. Many nights I've gone home thinking, 'I wish I'd stayed selling — I wouldn't have this pressure.' But you have to keep moving forward, even in the face of great uncertainty and doubts.

Steve Henderson is one of our most loved team members. He's quite a legend around our place. Let me tell you about Steve's persistence.

Steve's our office administrator. He's 30 years old, and this is his first full-time job. He is challenged by living with schizophrenia and is a slow learner in the traditional sense. (I say in the traditional sense because some of Steve's skills are remarkable. For example, we run a course called the Real Estate School of Excellence for newcomers to the industry. By morning tea on

Maintain your motivation

I'm not really into lots of material stuff, but the promise of a few rewards can give me the motivation to keep going. I continually remind myself of some of the rewards I'd like to give myself. I always have pictures around – of trips I want to take, things I'd like to do, places I'd like to live. Just looking at them generates excitement and provides energy.

Another way I maintain my motivation and passion is by reading about others who have achieved success. These stories inspire me to head for the next level, not in a greed-centred way, but more from the excitement of knowing what's possible. I'm always reading books, biographies,and magazines. I love *Fast Company* magazine for its articles about phenomenal people doing incredible things.

I also listen to my favourite music to give myself a blast of positive energy. I've got a compilation CD of my favourite songs in my car. Even though I only live three minutes' drive from work I can usually get one song in. It helps me arrive in the office pumped up and ready to go.

the first day, Steve will have remembered the names of all 50 participants!)

The story of how Steve came to work for us is a great lesson in persistence. Steve met one of my Associate Directors, James Dack, at a fundraiser. When he found out James worked in real estate, Steve decided to ask him for a job — despite his challenges, and lack of work experience.

When Steve told me the story later he recalled with pride, 'I asked James if he needed a hand because I thought real estate would be a great job.' James wanted to help him if at all possible. He told Steve to keep in touch because he might have some part-time work in the future. Though James's offer was genuine, he hadn't put any thought into what work he might be able to offer Steve.

I asked Steve when did he follow up James on his offer? 'The next day,' he said, as though it was a strange question to ask. 'But unfortunately James didn't have anything for me at the time.'

'Well I assume you followed him up some more Steve, because here you are,' I said.

'Of course I did,' he replied, again looking strangely at me as though it was the obvious thing to do. (As most managers know, there are so many people who ask for work one day and are never heard of again.)

'And when was the first time you called to follow up James?'

'Not long after,' he said.

'The next week?'

'Oh no,' he said, 'I called him six times a day, every day until something became available. I didn't want to miss out on a position.'

Steve's persistence, enthusiasm and excitement for life paid off, and he continues to be an inspiration to everyone on our team.

The laws of compound interest apply to all areas of life

Most people understand how compound interest works to increase their wealth. You put some money in the bank and a month later you're paid some interest. The next month you get interest on the original amount, plus interest on the interest. Your investment grows steadily, and eventually exponentially.

I think life works in a similar way. Some people call it karma. You invest the energy in being good to people and that good energy is returned to you with interest. You have more good energy to give out and even more good energy returns as a result.

So if you invest in your business every day by creating great customer service, giving recognition and rewards to your staff and creating a great working atmosphere, you'll quickly see your business prosper as a result.

You don't have to make big investments either and it's not only about spending money. Don't underestimate the cumulative effect of lots of little things. The smile you receive when you walk in. Answering the phone by the second ring. Keeping the washrooms clean and tidy. Caring for your customers often costs nothing.

Virtually all businesses have the same basic customer interactions. They meet customers, they show their wares, negotiate a deal and move on. It's what you do during these interactions that gives you the edge. It's the how you do it that makes the difference.

Think positive thoughts every moment

Accept the fact that your attitude creates the results you experience, both personally and professionally. So be more selective about what you read, what you listen to and who you spend time with. Make it a point to put positive thoughts into your mind every single day.

Dealing with obstacles, failure and rejection

Navigating your way past obstacles requires that you view them as a lesson, not as disastrous or something to be embarrassed about. Only the naive think that success will arrive without failure along the way. Failure is part of the journey — one of the most important parts.

When I look back over 20 years of my business, I have no doubt that my greatest learning experiences, and the times I grew into a far better business person, came about from experiences that would typically be classified as failures or rejections.

People often avoid failure at all costs (usually by not trying in the first place), but it should be embraced as a wonderful opportunity to learn and grow. Again, look for the gift in your situation.

Inevitably you will have some tough patches when you've screwed up or dropped the ball. So it helps to have some inspirational and positive-minded people to support you. They don't have to be part of your company; they can be friends, relatives or business colleagues. But it helps to have them all around you.

One of my biggest screw-ups occurred in the early days of my business. I had a good friend of mine working with me. I trusted him because not only was he a friend, but he had been very successful in his career. I found out 18 months later that he had been ripping me off financially.

He'd stolen $25,000 from me, which doesn't sound a lot today, but it was a hell of a lot when I had only been in business 18 months. We weren't really making any profit. At best we were breaking even. So this was an enormous challenge for me financially.

But I stayed positive and looked for the lesson. I had actually delegated the cheque signing and in retrospect I realised I shouldn't have. Following this incident, I totally re-evaluated every system from a financial perspective. We now run an extremely tight ship. We can account for every single cent and operate the business incredibly frugally. But if I hadn't had that 'failure', I wouldn't have received all the benefits derived from improving our financial systems.

If you don't ask the question, the answer's always no

One of our most profitable businesses is the Australasian Real Estate Conference (AREC). It's the largest real estate conference in the Southern Hemisphere and this year we'll have 1500 delegates from Australia, New Zealand, and even America. It all started with a throwaway comment I made one day eight years ago.

I used to go to the US regularly for small real estate workshops with some of the best agents in America. One time I was sitting at the Four Seasons in Chicago listening to these guys and sharing in their wisdom, and I thought to myself, 'How lucky am I to be here listening to how these people think and how they operate? I'd love to have my people back in the office hear this straight from the source.'

In the morning tea break I went up to the facilitator, Dr Fred Grosse, who was one of my early mentors, and said, 'Fred, I feel so privileged to be here and be invited to listen to you guys talk. The only thing I regret is that no-one else in my business can hear this. I wish these guys could come to Australia and talk to my team.'

It wasn't a serious suggestion — it was just a throwaway line. So I was a bit taken aback when Fred said, 'Well let's ask them.' I freaked out. I mean these are the top real estate agents in the world, making millions of dollar a year. I didn't want to waste their extremely valuable time. I tried to make some excuses, but

Fred wasn't having it. 'They might all be too busy,' he said, 'but you must give them the opportunity to say *yes*.'

So after the break Fred says, 'John's got a request.' I stood up, feeling very uncomfortable, and said, 'I'm bit embarrassed to ask this, but I just wondered whether anyone would be interested in one day coming to speak to my team in Australia?' I was bowled over with the response. All the heads in the room were nodding, and they said, 'We'd love to come.' I couldn't believe it. Something that was a pipe dream five minutes ago had suddenly started to materialise.

To cut a long story short, we agreed that in 12 months' time, six of them would come to Australia to talk to my team and I would pay for their airfares, accommodation and out of pocket expenses. Only trouble was, I couldn't really afford it. So I called up some friends in the industry and asked if they'd like to hear these guys and make a contribution to help me cover costs.

Word spread, and before long I had about 60 people attending and I covered half my costs. That was the beginning of AREC, and we kept building it from there. Nowadays we're the biggest real estate trainers in Australia and we get a dozen top real estate experts from around the world presenting every year.

Moving from dream to reality was just a matter of asking a question. Sure I had doubts — I didn't know how I could pay for it for starters — but if I hadn't given those agents the opportunity to say *yes*, then nothing would've happened. And once they'd said *yes*, all I had to do was work out how to pull it off.

So the next time you're in a café and you scribble down a great idea for your business or your life on a napkin, don't just leave it at that. It could be the seed of something great. Breathe some oxygen into your idea and see if you can give it life. Take a risk, and ask the question. Because the answer may well be yes.

4.

Are you fit for business?

Are you wondering why I've included a section on health and fitness in a book about creating a successful business? You might be tempted to skip over this chapter and go straight to the sections on sales or management. If you did, you'd be making a big mistake, because the simple fact is, you can't run a successful business without good health and lots of positive energy.

Good energy levels and an overall sense of physical and emotional wellbeing are the foundations you need to create a successful business. I'll discuss how the leader's energy has a positive effect on the whole team later in the book.

It's also important to remember that business is not an end in itself. You should be aiming to have a great business as one component of a great life. You can build a great business with lots of sales and zeros on the bank balance. But if your health is poor you've actually lost the game of life — you just have more money in the bank.

I believe business has three major outcomes: it's a vehicle for you to learn about yourself and life, it allows you to make a contribution to your community and the world, and it provides you with the funds to have an interesting and fun life.

Without good health you will never be able to fully achieve these outcomes. Why create a business if you're not able to reap the maximum benefits due to poor health or an early departure?

Many of you may have been neglecting your health for some time, not watching what you eat and not doing any regular exercise. Well don't worry. The good news is that most people can attain a state of great health in just 90 days. You might have been abusing your body for the past 10 or 15 years, but three months from today you can be a totally changed person. All it takes is a simple plan and a bit of discipline.

Food management

Obviously a big part of your health depends on what you eat. I don't like to use the word 'diet', because it has negative connotations of short-term fixes with no lasting results. Besides, people never stick to diets. I prefer the term food management. I look at healthy eating as the ongoing management of what you eat, how much you eat, and when you eat it.

First, let me tell you the good news. You can eat all the yummy stuff that you know is not good for you, just as long as you don't eat it too regularly and the rest of what you eat is healthy and fresh. I'll explain a little more about the permissible sins in a moment. To start, let's look at your staples.

Sit down and write up a list of healthy, tasty meals that you enjoy for breakfast, lunch and dinner. For example, at breakfast I have fresh fruit and yoghurt, porridge and banana, a soy smoothie made with fresh fruit, or wholemeal toast with Vegemite and sliced tomato. For a cooked breakfast, I like an egg white omelette with spinach and avocado.

List enough choices to keep your diet interesting, but not so many that it becomes confusing. I suggest about six to 10 options for each meal. Then every time you sit down for a meal you simply choose one of the dishes from your list. By using your list you ensure you're constantly fuelling your body with fresh, high quality, low fat foods.

I follow this food management plan from Monday to Friday with very few diversions. But when the working week's done I give myself a weekend pass. That is, I allow myself to eat whatever I want. Chinese, pizza, hamburgers, cinnamon donuts...anything goes. I treat myself to virtually anything I feel like.

It's important to note that even though I have the liberty to eat whatever I like, I don't pig out on junk food all weekend. I might treat myself to fish and chips, but I still end up eating a lot of meals from my list. And that's not just because I'm trying to be good, but because by sticking to healthy foods most of the time, your body naturally returns to a balanced state and you start to crave healthy alternatives.

I've also noticed that if I fuel up on quality food at most meals I'm less likely to feel like snacking on less nutritious foods like sweets or pastries in between.

I take a daily nutritional supplement, even though my diet is good. It's a sad reality that much of the food we eat is not as high in nutrients and vitamins as it was a generation ago, due to degradation of soil quality and pesticide use. A nutritional supplement is an inexpensive insurance policy, ensuring I receive my daily nutritional needs. I take a good quality multivitamin, co-enzyme Q10 and flaxseed oil each morning, but I suggest you consult a nutritionist or health expert to find out what is best for you.

My final suggestion is that you only eat until you feel two-thirds full. Overeating is one of the biggest health problems today. How did this come about? As kids many of us were told we couldn't leave the table until we'd finished everything on our plates. Sadly, many adults have continued with this habit and an epidemic of obesity is the result.

Throw away the menu

When I walk into a café for breakfast I almost never look at the menu because I already know my preferred choices. I can't remember a good café or restaurant that hasn't been able to create these in an instant. (If they can't, I simply choose the closest option on the menu and rarely return to that café!)

Exercise and flexibility

Deepak Chopra once said that he'd prefer to have a junk food diet with regular exercise, than a healthy diet and no exercise. This demonstrates how important one of the world's greatest experts on health and wellbeing considers exercise to be. Unfortunately, often the last exercise many people did was at high school or university some 20 or 30 years ago.

People resist doing exercise because they often consider it boring or unpleasant. Who hasn't heard a coach or PE teacher say 'no pain, no gain' at least once in their life? Sure if you're training for a first grade team you have to do the hard yards. But doing exercise simply to achieve a good quality of life can be (and should be) pleasurable and fun.

I encourage you to exercise at least three times a week, for 30 to 60 minutes. The trick is to find activities that you actually enjoy doing, and not do them too hard. Ayurveda (an ancient Indian form of medicine) teaches that once you get to a point of pain when exercising, it's probably doing you more harm than good (this is great news for most of you!). And clearly you're going to find it easier to stay fit if exercise is something you really enjoy doing, like playing tennis, surfing or throwing a Frisbee to your dog.

There are three elements of exercise you should consider: aerobic, strength and flexibility. Aerobic exercise builds up your cardiovascular system and includes running, bike riding and swimming — things that raise a sweat and can get you out of breath.

There are lots of studies that show resistance and strength exercise stimulates your hormonal system. So it doesn't just make you stronger, it actually has very profound, positive physiological impact on you.

But it's not enough to be fit and strong — you must be flexible as well. We've all seen the muscle men that walk out of the gym and claim to be fit and healthy, but can't touch their toes.

I really encourage people to combine all three elements in their exercise regime. Flexibility can include stretching before and after you exercise, yoga, Pilates or separate stretching sessions at home. But whatever you do, don't forget flexibility.

If you're just getting back into exercising it's easiest just to start doing something — anything — and build up from there. Take a walk for a couple of laps around the block where you work at lunchtime (preferably before you eat lunch). I've got a habit, that unless something is on the fourth floor or above, I always use the stairs. Little things like that can make a really big difference.

I prefer to exercise in the morning, before I start work. There are some physiological benefits, but it's also good time management. How many good intentions of going to the gym or pool after work founder on an offer to have a drink or see a movie with a friend instead?

Sleep

It's essential to get the right amount of good quality sleep every night to allow your body to recuperate and recharge. Different people need different amounts of sleep, but between six and eight hours is enough for most of us. Make sure you get the right amount every night.

The sleep you get prior to midnight is of a much higher quality than the sleep you get after midnight. It really pays to get a couple of hours of shuteye in before midnight if you can.

Some people are not naturally as good sleepers as others. Often when people don't sleep well it's because they've gotten into bad habits that retard their ability to sleep easily. So it can be beneficial to create your own bedtime ritual to help you get to sleep soundly.

For some people it may be doing some exercise before sleep, but for others that will actually stimulate them. For still others it may be a hot bath with some lavender oil, or putting a few drops of lavender oil on the pillow. Trial a few methods and see which one works best for you.

Finally, don't eat within two hours of going to sleep. It takes between two and four hours for your body to digest a meal properly. You must allow your body to digest your dinner fully before you go to sleep.

Meditation

By eating right, doing regular exercise and getting a good night's sleep you're well on your way to top physical shape. And of course you'll be feeling great as well. But I'd urge you to do something more for your psychological and spiritual wellbeing. I'm talking about meditation.

Now for all the cynics and sceptics, who have visions of flowing robes, beads and incense in the boardroom, let me tell you how I started Transcendental Meditation or TM.

In 1991 I was really feeling under pressure. My business was growing fast and at that point had momentarily moved beyond my control. My staff numbers had doubled (albeit to only about

15 people, but nonetheless) and experts were saying the property market was crashing. I was in a state of high stress to say the least.

I noticed one of my salespeople at the time was looking particularly relaxed, calm and confident as he went about his work. He also noticed I was looking exactly the opposite. 'How are you feeling?' he asked as though on cue.

'Bit stressed,' I responded with a high degree of understatement.

'You should check out TM,' he suggested. 'I've been doing it for a few weeks and it's changed my life.'

Well I don't know about you, but my ears prick up immediately whenever anyone uses that phrase to describe something. Changed his life! I needed some of that.

So I feigned vague interest, being careful not to let the more sensitive me show through my macho exterior (long since discarded). It turned out the meditation centre was in a big terrace house less than 50 metres from our office. In fact, it was just seven doors away.

I'm not a terribly religious person (in the traditional sense), but this TM thing worried me. It sounded like it bordered on some new form of cult, and that was certainly not what I was after. But I was intrigued sufficiently to make an enquiry (with the echo of 'it changed my life' ringing in my ears).

On my first call I was so nervous I hung up the phone after it rang twice. I called back and hung up again after a few rings.

After several feeble attempts to contact the centre I was caught by surprise when the phone was answered before I heard a ring tone (obviously the disgruntled receptionist on the other end of the line was looking for swift vengeance). So I did the only sensible thing I could. I hung up again.

I felt terribly guilty about hanging up in someone's ear, so in a moment of courage I decided to walk down the road and visit the centre in person. It was a beautiful day, and like a scene out of a biblical movie, a perfect ray of sunshine was focused on the front garden of the terrace.

I knocked on the door and a man opened it. 'Hello. Could I see Thom Knoles if he's available. My name is John McGrath,' I said.

'Welcome John. Come in. I'm Thom Knoles and I've been expecting you,' he replied.

That freaked me out. How on earth could he have known I was coming to visit?

'How do you mean?' I stammered with a confused smile.

'I've been aware of your business growing rapidly and I saw you in the newspaper recently. You looked stressed in the photo and I figured it wouldn't be long before you looked me up for some help.'

Wow. I can tell you I was impressed with his ability to read my body language from a photo. And I was also put at ease by his appearance. The flowing, purple robes and grey beard I had envisaged were actually a beautifully hand-tailored Italian suit and smart slip-on business shoes.

Thom took me inside and made me a refreshing cup of green tea and we spoke about life, business, health and many other things that interested me greatly. I booked in to start my TM training the next morning.

At the first session it took all of about 15 minutes for me to feel a surge of powerful energy and a simultaneous, but almost contradictory, feeling of calm. I had never experienced anything like this before, and it was the most wonderful sensation.

I won't go into the detail of the process here. I think it's more important to relay to you the fears and prejudices I had to overcome before I could get into meditation. For most of us it's not getting the information that's hard. It's taking action on the things that hold us back.

A brief footnote to the Thom Knoles story: Thom and I became the closest of friends, so close in fact that he asked me to be his best man at his wedding a few years later. I continue to practise TM and reap the rewards in business and in life some 12 years later.

Inner calm

The biggest benefit I derive from meditation is inner calm. The world can be a chaotic place at times, and the world of business is no exception. In the midst of this chaos we are being bombarded by so many thoughts every minute. Meditation is simply sitting quietly and releasing these thoughts so you can find a place of inner calm.

In this calm space a natural process of mental spring cleaning occurs. We can store hurts and stresses in our subconscious for years, even decades, without realising it. Sometimes I'll be meditating and a memory of a comment someone made years ago will spring into my mind. It might be something a colleague had said five years ago.

I'm often not aware that it's an unresolved issue, but then it just pops into my consciousness. And then, after a short while, the tension just dissipates, and it's gone. I feel relieved and much lighter. I have no idea how it works, and I don't care, because I know it does. It's a gradual process, day in, day out, clearing your subconscious of anything that's no longer useful for it.

Meditating twice a day is ideal, but to be honest, I usually do it once a day. Even once or twice a week is beneficial. Like anything good for you, something is better than nothing. Each session normally lasts 15 to 20 minutes. It's not difficult to learn. You can probably pick it up in half an hour.

Your life foundations

Make exercising, meditating, reviewing your goals and eating properly the foundations of your life. If things start getting out of control, go back to your foundations and see if there's something you can do to get back on track. Maybe you need a brief walk, a little time alone to gather your thoughts, a glass of water or a quick read of your goals.

As well as spiritual outcomes, your meditation practice will have many great pay-offs in business. You'll be able to stay calmer in stressful situations. Your mind will be less cluttered, your thought processes clearer and your heart rate lower, leaving you better able to focus on the business at hand.

Stress management

To reach your optimum performance in business (and in life) you must learn to minimise stress. There will be many crises and challenges on the road to success and they're more difficult to deal with if you're always stressed out. Creativity rarely comes out of stress and it's hard work to improve your business if you're constantly in struggle mode.

In my early twenties I was so stressed out I got ulcers. I had just started my business, it was financially challenging and I felt that I didn't have enough experience. Sometimes I wished that I'd stayed working for somebody else. Everything changed when I began to see every problem, setback and challenge as a gift rather than a disaster.

You see, stress is caused by your response to events and situations. It's not so much the event or situation that causes you stress, but what you make that event or situation mean to you. For example, some sportspeople play their best game of the season in the grand final. They're excited about the prospect of winning and eager to show how well they can do. Other players have a shocker. They feel under a great amount of pressure to perform and doubt whether they're up to the task.

So by changing what you make an event or situation mean to you allows you to reduce the stress involved. My advice is to try to see the gift in everything. Ask yourself, what good is going to come out of this? What's the reward in this situation? If you look carefully, you'll always find a gift.

There's a gift in even the biggest calamity. Your spouse leaves, you feel terrible and wonder whether life's worth living. But look at it another way and you can see your partner did you a favour by leaving. The relationship obviously wasn't right for either of you. Now you're free to create a better relationship with someone more suitable. Yes there will be pain, but if you look for the reward all sorts of possibilities arise.

Or you might find yourself short of money, unable to pay your bills. The situation seems dire, but still there is a gift. You recognise you need to be more disciplined with money so you write a budget. Having no money is a humbling experience so your learn humility. You realise that you have to take your finances more seriously, so you move to a whole new level of performance in your career to ensure this never happens again.

The beauty of seeing the gift is that by choosing to focus on the positive outcome in any event or situation you can rid yourself of stress — starting right now! Anything that used to be a problem in your life is now no longer a problem. Rejection? No problem! If I ring up 10 prospects and they all say they don't want to do business with me, no problem. I'm now that much closer to the eleventh prospect that is going to say 'Yes, I'd love to do business with you.'

You're not John Wayne

Don't think you have to tough it out and solve all your problems yourself like some John Wayne character in a Western. The old adage that a problem shared is a problem halved is a good one. Sometimes it's hard to see the gift in a situation. That's when you need a different perspective from a mentor, coach, peer, best friend or spouse.

I've found coaches and mentors a big help for working through my issues. I'll walk in and tell my business coach if I'm challenged by an issue. So he'll talk me through it, and often his calm response, and ability to put my problem into perspective, will have a very deep impact on me.

I walk out of the room lighter, happier, thinking this is not such a big issue after all. But the issue hasn't changed. Nothing changed in that 15 minutes, except my way of looking at the issue. And when you see a different way of looking at it, you change the energy associated with it.

Balance

Often people get so immersed in their business their lives become unbalanced. Business is a great tool for learning, personal growth and for wealth creation, which are all important parts of life. But life is about living, it's not just about business.

Surely you don't get to the end of your life and look back and regret not spending more time in the office. I think most people would look back and say, 'I wish I'd spent some more quiet time by myself or with my closest friends. I wish I'd spent some more time walking in the park and enjoying nature. I wish I'd picked up my kids from school more often.'

Remember, there's always going to be some pain in life. I choose the pain of discipline, to create a balanced life that I love living, rather than the pain of regret of a life half lived. Because the pain of regret is a hell of a lot greater.

People often overwork because of the beliefs they have around hard work and success. It's a common belief that the harder you work, the more you achieve. That's certainly what I believed in the early days of my business. I believed 'if you work 60 hours, and you want to improve your performance, go to 80. Go to 80 and you want to do a bit better, go to 90'.

My belief was that if a client of mine saw me on the weekend in a tracksuit not working, it would reflect badly on my business. Before long my work became all consuming. I was getting worn out and very boring. So I had to shift that belief. I said to myself that clients want to deal with interesting people that have balanced lives, they don't want to deal with boring workaholics.

I still do believe that hard work is one of the factors that will bring you success. But I also believe that building other interests outside of your work and keeping your life in balance make you far more effective at work. Also, staff don't want to work for bosses who are workaholics, in poor health or are poor role models. People actually aspire to work with bosses that have got their lives together.

You know your life is in balance when you're happy, financially secure, emotionally stable, physically fit, loving to your fellow man and at peace with God.

Balancing career and family

Pauline Goodyer is one of the Associate Directors of McGrath and one of our top salespeople. Since she had her first child she's been working online and we hardly ever see her in the office. Yet Pauline's career has never missed a beat. She hasn't had to compromise her family life and she's still an incredibly efficient and successful real estate salesperson.

I'll let her tell you in her own words how she manages to balance her career and family:

'I still enjoy what I'm doing and still work to the same ability I worked at before I had my baby. But now time management is much more important. When I'm at work, I'm very focused on working and I rely on my personal assistant a lot more than I used to. If there are problems at home with my daughter and I have to be there, I can work online at home quite easily. I'm only in the office for about 20% of my work time.

'My day has lock-out times for work, plus lock-out times for personal activities. When I'm running auction campaigns, which usually run for a month, all my appointments are locked-out in my diary. The same goes for my personal life. Whereas I used to ring up the hairdressers and go in whenever I could fit it in, now I book in advance. I do the same with family holidays.

'I started working within two weeks of having my baby. One sale I had going at the time was for a famous ex-model who had been trying to sell her house for three years. We met when I was heavily pregnant and she had no hesitation in appointing me. She had children of her own and could understand exactly where I was at.

'I sold the house over the Internet to a family from Washington, USA. It all worked out quite well because I could communicate with them via email when I was up in the middle of the night feeding my baby.

'The main reason why people move houses is usually because of their family — whether it's an upgrade or a downsize. So clients are actually very understanding when you have children of your own. I think they relate a lot better to you.'

It's about life

I came across this quote well over a decade ago. It made such a big impact on me because I realised that's where I wanted to be, but I wasn't there yet. So I copied it and laminated it. I pull it out every few months and I think about where I am right now and how much closer I've moved to this goal.

'I'm at a stage of my life where I don't need to prove anything. I'm just doing what I want to do, and it's a great place to be. I'm working at a feverish pace, I'm having such a good time! But my goals are no longer just geared to success. Now it's about my life, about living, about time away from work, about my wife who I love so much.'

PART TWO

You+business

5.

The five worst business mistakes and how to avoid them

One of the ways I've achieved success is by studying successful people and businesses. I've then adapted their strategies to suit my life and business. Another route to success is to study businesses that have failed, find out why, and not do that! Here are some lessons I've learnt about what not to do in business.

The five worst business mistakes

1. Lack of clarity.

2. Fighting fires rather than building firebreaks.

3. No plan.

4. No accountability.

5. Poor time management.

1. Lack of clarity

You'd think most business owners would be very clear about two things: where they're headed and how they plan to get there. In other words, their goals and strategies. Yet I'm amazed how few businesspeople have total clarity on these basic business foundations.

First work out your goals. Imagine how your business would look if it were exactly the way you wanted it. Imagine for a moment that in three years you've taken your business where you want it to go. What could you tell me about the business at that point?

How many people do you employ? What's your turnover and what's your profit? What are your key revenue streams? What regions are you operating in?

The answers to these key questions form the basis of your goals. Now you must devise the concrete actions that you'll need to take to attain these goals. These actions form the basis of your strategies.

Why don't all business owners have clarity about their goals and strategies? I believe it's because many businesses have failed at goal-setting in the past. They have set themselves goals and then failed to achieve them for one reason or another. But instead of using that experience constructively and refining their strategies or reassessing their goals, they often decide to give up on goal-setting altogether. Mistake number one.

2. Fighting fires rather than building firebreaks

One of the most important business books I've ever read is *The E-Myth* by Michael Gerber. It taught me that one of the keys to success in business is your ability to establish effective systems to run your business, and then spend most of your time working 'on' your business rather than 'in' your business. Stop being an employee and start being an owner.

Because most people never grasp this simple concept, they rarely have time to work on key business foundation stones, such as their business plan, marketing strategy, talent recruitment and systems development. This is what I call 'building firebreaks'. It's the big picture work that lays the groundwork for future success.

Many business owners spend too much time on the nitty-gritty operations of their business i.e. 'fighting fires'. It may seem a more compelling use of your time. These tasks also often appear more heroic: deal making, fixing up complaints or motivating employees. They usually give you quick wins and adrenalin jolts — instant gratification.

Fighting fires is also easier because it usually requires reacting to outside events or actions rather than the harder work of pro-actively taking action on things that will establish future prosperity. It's certainly important to devote time to fighting fires, but it's crucial to ration part of your time (further down the track, most of your time) to building firebreaks. Otherwise you'll end up fighting fires for the rest of your business life.

A shift from technician to entrepreneur

In essence it's a shift from technician to entrepreneur, from salesperson to business owner. After I first read *The E-Myth* I sat down with my business coach and we discovered I was spending far too much time in the business. I loved selling and I also loved dealing with operational stuff or fighting fires. But I realised that to catapult my business to the next level I needed to start building some firebreaks.

My coach asked, 'What do you fear about giving up selling to give you more time to work on strategic planning?' One of my big fears was that the business would falter if I stopped selling. At that time a lot of the business was based on my personal sales effort. My coach suggested there might be a small temporary drop-off, but I couldn't let that stop me.

So I made some rules to give me more time to start working on the business. Firstly, I always attended sales appointments with another of our agents. Secondly, we created a dialogue so when a client asked if I'd personally be selling their property, I'd say up front that the key role I'd be playing would be establishing a strategy with them right now. 'Then I'll have Jamie here, who is an expert in this area, take over. I've asked her to come to this meeting because she actually knows far more buyers in this price range than I do. But I believe I can add value up front, here and now, and I'm only a phone call away if you want a second opinion.'

Finally I set up a series of expectations for my agents as to their role: They'd do research and brief me before meeting the client. Afterwards, I'd expect them to prepare a presentation and some documentation for me to look over. So everybody was clear on what was expected.

Far from my fear of the business falling apart coming true, I found that nothing missed a beat. In fact, within a year business had increased by over 50%. The same thing happened when I stopped auctioning. In my mind, I had to keep auctioning until the day I died, because if I stopped maybe the clients would stop coming. But when I did stop auctioning, business actually doubled!

I was working five days a week in the office and then auctioning on Saturdays and Sundays. So by stopping selling and auctioning, I was able to spend far more time focusing on the business. I also found I have my best ideas on my days off!

Talk to your Scarer to overcome fears

I've named one of the self-doubting voices in my head The Scarer. You know, it's the one that comes up with all the catastrophic scenarios: 'Look out John – if you stop being a salesperson, the business will fail!' Never let The Scarer stop you from doing things. Instead, talk to The Scarer and say: 'Okay Scarer, what could go wrong if I try this?' Write down all the things The Scarer would say and simply create a strategy to deal with each one.

By reducing the time spent fighting fires I've also got far more balance in my life. Not only have I made gains in my personal life by having more harmony and balance, I'm also a far better businessperson by concentrating my time on working on the business from more of a helicopter view rather than from the trenches.

3. No plan

Very few businesses start without a business plan. Almost none. However, very few businesses get their plan right at the beginning. In fact, almost none. Therefore the ongoing evolution of your business plan and strategies is far more important than your initial plan. Rarely do I come across a business or a salesperson that can articulate their strategy, or, better still, provide a written summary of their goals, strategy, key milestones, tactics and likely challenges and obstacles. Knowing these things and refining them constantly is a key factor in successful businesses.

A business plan's success is inversely proportional to its length

In 15 years of business we've had literally dozens of business plans. My first plans were long and detailed. More recently I've found that a business plan's success is inversely proportional to its length. The key to a good business plan is brevity. Most people have a natural resistance to any document longer than one page. These usually end up in a drawer somewhere. They're too hard to read or you never have time.

Therefore, our business has a plan that consists of less than one page for each business unit. The plan is in bullet-point form for ease of reference and is constantly modified depending on changes to the market, new directions agreed on by the management team, ideas from our employees, or just plain intuition.

A good strategic plan is one you can fit on one PowerPoint slide and take in at a glance. It's easily understood by your team and your managers know it by heart. About five to seven points is best. This doesn't mean that you can't have more detail in another document. But first and foremost you must have a useable document that your people can read daily if they want to.

Be realistic about what you're trying to achieve. You don't have to have 500 goals, you can have just six. I have a one-pager on outcomes, and a one-pager on strategy. One has the outcomes I want to achieve in the next year in business and the other is the ten most important things I'm going to do to get there.

Making a plan

Your challenge is to bridge the gap which exists between where you are now and the goals you intend to reach. Developing the plan is actually laying out the structure of events that have to occur for you to achieve each goal. Divide your plan into a sequence of easy-to-do steps. If you fail to reach your goal, divide again.

4. No accountability

Lack of accountability is one of the main reasons people and businesses rarely rise to their potential. When people set their goals they rarely have a mechanism to have their progress towards those goals checked by someone else. Business owners establish certain outcomes with their managers or employees, yet often fail to monitor their progress or hold them accountable for the results.

Here's a typical scenario: a sales manager sits down with one of his salespeople. 'Let's set up our goals for the next 90 days. What do you think is achievable?', which is followed by a conversation and eventually an agreement on the next quarter's goals. Sounds simple, so what could go wrong?

The first problem is that managers rarely have an honest conversation around expectations, responsibility and accountability. A good manager would take some time to discuss the likely challenges and obstacles to achieving the outcome, and be very clear about what happens in the event that the outcomes are not met.

For example a manager might say, 'In the event that at any stage you get derailed and are having trouble staying on track to achieve these goals, here's what I expect...' The manager should leave no uncertainty as to who's responsible for achieving the results and what to do if there's a problem. This honest, up-front exchange greatly increases the prospects of outcomes being delivered.

The next problem is that all too often the next time a sales manager has an in-depth discussion about the outcomes is at the end of the quarter. It's much more effective to establish key milestones leading up to the ultimate goal, and schedule regular pit stops to check progress. This ensures that any problems or variations to the pre-agreed plan are caught at an early stage.

5. Poor time management

Good time management is a key component of success, and poor time management is one of the major reasons for failure. Most businesses have the motivation, talent and opportunities, but they waste too much time on things that are irrelevant. You must work out what your most important tasks are, and then make sure you have enough time to do them.

Each person is gifted with 24 hours each day and the thing that sets people apart is what they do within that time. On any given day you can fill your time with stuff — some important and some not important — or you can focus with laser beam concentration on the five most critical things to drive your business forward. It's your choice.

So what do I do with a To Do list with 100 items staring me in the face? I decide which are the five most important tasks on the list — the tasks that will have the most significant impact and will progress the business today (typically not the easiest ones by the way) — and I do them first. Once I've finished those tasks I move onto the five next most important tasks, and so on.

Is that hard? At first, yes. But when you get good at it, it becomes empowering, liberating and incredibly effective.

Will you upset some people in the process of maintaining this focus and concentration of energy? Yes, no doubt some people will be put out. But you have to work out your priorities. Do you continually attempt to make everyone happy and try to get everyone to like you, or do you build a world-class business that makes a difference? It's up to you to decide.

Designer time management techniques

I've been inspired by the time management techniques of two great designers. Giorgio Armani does only eight things a day. He works eight hours each day, plus an hour for lunch. He only has eight things he needs to do each day. If he doesn't finish a task in the hour, he moves it to the next day. He's working simultaneously on eight projects, but only eight. Imagine if you were to adopt this practice how much you might get done.

You look at most people's To Do list and they have 74 items on it. At the end of the week, they've got 84, and most of the original 74 are probably still there. So it makes a lot of sense to prioritise down to the key tasks. If you batch all your phone calls and emails into an hour at the beginning of the day and an hour at the end of the day and you take out an hour for lunch, you're left with six to eight hours. What is the best most productive use for you and your business for those six to eight hours?

At the great designer Phillipe Starck's office everyone starts work at 9.00 a.m., but they don't take any calls until 1.00 p.m. There's an answering machine in the office which says, 'The morning is for thinking, the afternoon is for doing. We're thinking at the moment, please leave a message.' The staff clearly understands that the morning is for design, thinking and collaboration, and they don't want to be disturbed.

Many businesspeople would be amazed how much they could get done if they set up simple time management systems such as these. As part of my current system I have all my meetings for the week on Mondays. I fit in all my internal meetings, client meetings and other key appointments. I meet with my leadership team and review their businesses, performance and outcomes, and look at the strategies.

The rest of the week I spend time on my key projects, visiting my other offices, meeting with my board if necessary, strategising and so on. Typically I get into the office between 6.30 a.m. and 7.00 a.m. and that gives me at least four to five hours to prepare for the day and follow up on yesterday's tasks.

6.

The essential mechanics of any world-class business

Are you better at running a business or building a business? Small businesspeople usually have plenty of entrepreneurial flair, enthusiasm and energy. Building business is their forte — that's why they choose to start their own business.

It's running a business where they often find themselves lacking. There's no point going out there and marketing up a storm if you haven't sorted out your order fulfilment or the phone's about to be cut off because no-one paid the bill. Before you grow your business you need to get your operations and systems running smoothly. Here are a few tips to get you started.

Invest in advance of growth

I'm a big believer in reverse engineering. In a business sense this means imagining where you want your business to be, and then mentally backtracking through all the steps you would have to take to get there. Once you know what the steps are, you can create strategies to achieve them. But begin with the end in mind.

We had a meeting recently. We decided one of our goals was to increase business over the next five years. We decided that we wanted to increase our profit by about 500% over the next seven years. So we asked ourselves: 'How would our business look if it were doing five times the revenue and profit? What would the people look like? What would the energy of the office be? What would the systems need to be? What technology would be in place?' Once we knew the answers to these questions, it was just a matter of putting those things in place.

The trick is you can't wait until you get there to put them in place. You actually have to put them in place in advance. This is one of the great lessons that I have learned: you must invest in advance of growth. For a lot of entrepreneurs, that's really tough because there's a degree of risk involved in putting in place the infrastructure before it's actually needed. But you just have to do it.

I remember in 1997 the highest-paid employee in the business was earning $80,000 (not including sales staff). My business coach told me, 'You might have to recruit a high-calibre person.' OK, so I thought I might have to pay them $100,000. He said, 'What about $200,000?' That comment scared me to death. I thought 'Hang on a second — I can get three people for that.' He said, 'No, you have to understand at times you need to hire higher-calibre people if you're going to grow the business.'

After I got over the initial shock I ended up hiring someone for about $180,000, and the business did grow as a result. In fact it grew faster than ever before. But I had to take a leap of faith. And I had to be pushed to take it because it wasn't an easy decision. But the business never looked back.

Getting organised - systems are the answer

Time is your most precious commodity — don't waste it. Streamline your business to maximise your outcomes in the minimum time. It all comes down to systems. Look at McDonald's. They've built their empire by creating simple yet effective systems.

To get you started here are four key systems that you can implement this week:

1. Key meeting agendas

Most business and salespeople have regular key meetings, whether it's a weekly sales meeting, biannual think-tank or monthly team meeting. Most of the topics you will discuss remain the same from meeting to meeting. By having pro-forma agendas for each of your regular meetings you save time by keeping everyone focused on the matter at hand.

2. To Do list and key projects list

Everywhere I go I carry a To Do list with all the activities I've got to get through today. My key projects list encompasses all the major tasks I'm working on. In an ideal world all the actions on my daily To Do list are progressing my key projects, as opposed to dealing with crises. Keep a centralised list of all your tasks, goals and projects.

3. Key project folders and meeting folders

Every key project on the list has its own folder, where I collect relevant information and ideas. For each of my meetings (e.g. management, executive, team leaders, board meeting, etc) I also have an information folder. If something comes in that I want to discuss at the board meeting, I just slip it in the board meeting folder. When I'm getting ready for the meeting, all the items I want to discuss with the board are right there.

4. A series of in-trays

You need some in-trays to quickly capture important information that you'd like to refer to later. For example, I have a 'reading' in-tray. I don't start flicking through a magazine when it comes in. I put it in the reading tray, and if I'm going on a flight later in the week, I grab the contents of my reading tray, so I can read it on the plane.

5. One page business plan for each part of your business

I stress one page, because it means you've got to develop clarity to distil it. Also if it's more than one page, it probably won't get read. One page you can take in at a glance. If you have a small business, you might want to have a one page plan for each part of your business e.g. a one-page marketing plan, one-page sales plan, one-page operational and technology plan, etc. But one page, no more.

Fine-tuning your systems

Have a look at your business. Where's it working well? Where's it not working so well? Use your intuition. Query your staff. Ask your customers. Ring up a customer and say, 'I'd really appreciate your feedback on how it's been to do business with us?' A ten-minute phone call could be worth a million dollars to you down the track, based on the feedback you get.

Once you know where your business isn't working you have to go in and develop a system to make it work. Keep your systems simple, and remember to never let perfect get in the way of better (more on this later). Don't wait until you find a totally foolproof system — just start with something. Perhaps a short checklist of performance standards for the team members. Get some feedback. Have a few little focus groups and improve it as you go.

At some stage you might need help from an outside consultant. We often bring in consultants for specific projects. When managers are often working in the business, especially in small businesses, they rarely give themselves the opportunity — and sometimes they don't have the expertise — to take a look at the business from the outside and then restructure it if necessary. You might want to consider hiring someone to do that for you.

Top 10 time management strategies

It's easy to let your day fill up with stuff: attending appointments, answering emails and returning phone calls. But when it's time to go home you look back and think, 'I actually didn't do anything today that's going to change the face of this business.'

Good time management is one of the keys to high achievement. It's really about working out what your core activities are and building your schedule around them. If you create a solid schedule and work hard every day at staying on it, success is almost guaranteed to follow.

Here are my top 10 time management strategies:

1. Live your life in day-tight compartments

This is a great tip I picked up from one of Dale Carnegie's books. What he means is, only focus on what you have to do today. Aside from a quick glance in my diary to see what I have to prepare for the coming week, I never look beyond today.

Why? Because you can get distracted and even overwhelmed. If you look at your diary and you've got 12 meetings tomorrow, 12 meetings the next day, and so on, it's easy to feel snowed under. So I just focus on today's meetings, and the outcomes I'd like. At the end of the day I can have a good night's sleep knowing I'll take care of tomorrow's meetings tomorrow.

2. Develop a Morning Ritual – get momentum early

I've learned that if I have a non-productive morning, I'll end up having a lousy day. To avoid this, develop a Morning Ritual and start building positive momentum from the moment you step out of bed. Do something productive in the first hour or two after you wake up: take some exercise first thing, listen to an uplifting CD on the way to work, have breakfast with one of your top staff or a new recruit, or hold a morning meeting with your key managers.

3. Have an Ideal Week in place

By creating an Ideal Week you block out time to work on the core activities that will move your business forward. Fit all your other activities in around them. By working hard every day to stay on your schedule you develop consistency and achieve more.

Here's an example of my Ideal Week. At the top are my focus activities. These are my key roles in the business.

My ideal week

Focus activities:

- Strategy
- Create Energy
- Clear Energy
- Talent Management
- Build World-class Brand
- Build Relationships

Monday

8.00 - 9.00am	Sales Meeting – Eastern Suburbs
9.00 - 10.00am	Executive Team – Eastern Suburbs
10.00 - 11.00am	Management Team – Eastern Suburbs
11.00 - 12.00 noon	Residential Sales Management Team
12.00 - 6.00pm	Appointments/outside meetings

Tuesday

Visit regional offices

Wednesday

Visit regional offices

Thursday

Monthly business reviews

Quarterly review meetings

Project review and update meetings as required

Friday

Prepare for all Monday meetings

KPI Review

Strategy development and review

Speech preparation for next week

Board report and board papers

Quarterly/monthly review

Reading

4. Super Seven outcomes each day, week and month

Create a list of the top seven outcomes you want to achieve this month, this week and today. Obviously there's going to be a large degree of operational stuff on today's list. This week you should be moving some significant strategies forward. This month you should be moving seven major outcomes of your business forward. Start each month, week and day with your Super Seven outcomes.

5. Chunk your tasks into 30-60 minute bites

Chunk down major tasks and projects into manageable 30–60 minute bites. People often put off big tasks by saying, 'This will take me six hours, so when I get six hours free I'll do it.' But guess what? You never get six hours free, and it never gets done. Chunk it down into twelve 30-minute bites and put them in your diary over the next month.

6. Master the 'one minute telephone call'

Telephone and email are powerful communication tools, but they can also be enormous time wasters. Most businesspeople, and certainly most salespeople, spend the majority of their life on the phone. So you need to become expert at getting off the phone quickly, while still getting and giving all the necessary information.

Think about returning a phone call. I could say, 'Hi Sue, it's John McGrath. How are you? Great to talk to you. What have you been up to? Blah, blah, blah...' Or I could say, 'Hi Sue, it's John McGrath. I'm returning your call. How can I help you this morning?' This is going to get a direct response and possibly get me in and out in 60 seconds.

Bob Wolff from the US is one of the best real estate salespeople on the planet. To train himself to make quick phone calls he used an eggtimer. As soon as he was connected, he'd turn it upside down and he would give himself 60 seconds to get in and out of the phone call and get what he needed or provide the information his customer wanted.

7. Determine and eliminate the five most common distractions

List all the distractions you have during your day that take you off track and waste your time. Look at your list and identify your top five time wasters. Work out how you can eliminate these things. Is there someone in the office that continually drops in on you? You need to say to them, 'Jason, you know I love you to death, but you come into my office 10 times a day and it distracts me from my work. Is it OK if we meet up after work and you tell me about everything that's been happening then?'

8. Say NO to things that aren't important

This is one of life's great challenges. Many people spend much of their lives saying *yes* to things that either aren't important or they don't want to do. Figure out what's important in your life, what's important in your business and say YES! to those things with passion and enthusiasm. To everything else, just say NO.

9. Be specific about outcomes and issues

When I'm in a meeting or conversation, one of the things I'll often say is, 'So what are we trying to achieve here?' or 'What are the specific outcomes we need to address?' It cuts the waffle and everyone gets straight to the point. Develop some dialogue that helps you and everyone else get specific about what decisions need to be made right now.

10. Never leave the scene of a decision without taking action

When you've got to make a decision, decide to decide. Just do it. People get paralysed by the fear of making a wrong decision and meanwhile the whole business comes to a halt. To get beyond that, just recognise that a certain percentage of your decisions will be incorrect. However, it's more dangerous not to make a decision than it is to make a few incorrect decisions (which you can almost always fix later anyway).

Decide to decide

Anthony Robbins once said in one of his seminars that: 'We must remember that every moment we're alive, a new set of choices, a new set of actions and a new set of results are merely a decision or two away. Ultimately, it's our decisions and actions, not the conditions of our lives, that determine our destiny.'

The right people in the right places

All we need to do is get the right people, in the right places, with the right plan and the right systems.

Creating the right structure for your business is crucial. It always starts with the right people in the right places. You can have the best business model in the world, but if you have the wrong people, or the right people in the wrong place, you won't achieve your goals.

Right from the outset, put the effort in to create good structures. Because as you evolve from a technician to an entrepreneur, if you have a poor structure you'll get too caught up in administration, and end up burning out.

Before you take your business to the next level, make sure you have bulletproof systems in place for sales, marketing and finance. This allows you to grow with a minimum amount of stress and strain.

When you've got the right structure and systems in place you can move from working in the business to working *on* the business. You're actually running a team of people that are each reporting up to you about what's happening in their area, which frees you up to focus on the big picture.

That's how I see my job role. I add value to the business by helping my managers develop strategies and deal with issues, without necessarily working on the issues myself.

In any business there are three key roles: sales, marketing and operations. And even if you're a one-person operation you need to create the right structure from the outset. On my first organisational chart my name was on each of the three key roles. I was in effect head of marketing, head of sales and head of operations.

But even if you have a small business, create an organisational chart and fill in a name for every position. If your name's in every box, that's fine. Then ask yourself: 'If I were to build my team in the near future, what would be the key position they could fill that would free me up?' Maybe you'd recruit someone in operations to free you up to work more in sales. Or maybe you'd say, 'Sales is not my bag — I need to recruit an expert in sales and marketing to take us forward.'

Check your KPIs regularly

KPI stands for Key Performance Indicator. These are the most important measures you keep track of to see how your business is going. They allow you to feel the pulse of the business quickly and regularly, and keep everything on track.

For example, some of our KPIs are the number of sales listings and leases signed, the number of page views on our website, our market share in each suburb and how much cash we have in the bank.

How often should you check them? That depends on your business. Years ago I read about Donald Trump and his casinos. Because cash was coming in constantly, hour by hour, and being deposited into bank accounts, he used to get hourly bank statements. Now that's obviously an extreme example, but it certainly woke me up to the importance of keeping close track of what's important.

For the KPIs I mentioned above, we track them weekly and discuss them at our weekly management meetings. You must work out what your business's KPIs are, and how often to check them. Ideally you should find a way of having someone report them to you, so you don't spend the whole time chasing them yourself.

The best way to track and compare your KPIs is on a graph, because numbers in isolation don't mean much. But when you see a visual representation of your KPIs you can easily identify and track trends. I'm a great believer in graphing results so you can immediately see where your business is growing or not growing. It puts everything in perspective.

Internal communication

One of the most effective forms of internal communication is email. I like it because it's so fast. I think that's what email is all about: fast, seamless, direct communication. The average time it takes me to send an email is 10 seconds. I don't bother about spelling, punctuation and layout too much (unless it's a sales presentation of course). It's really about the response: what's the answer to this question I've got?

Zap Emails

I use Zap Emails to keep the positive energy flowing around the office. They're quick emails giving the recipient some positive feedback. I find out who's doing well from feedback from my executive team, our sales reports or customers' comments, and I type out a quick note of praise and encouragement.

I'm committed to sending five every day, but I can send up to 20. I usually send them first thing in the morning so they're sitting in my team member's inbox when they arrive. It gives them a little zap of positive energy to start the day.

Group voicemail

We also have voicemail and sometimes we do group voicemails. I might do a voicemail message to all the staff in one department, or the entire staff.

I picked up this group voicemail idea from Gail Kelly, head of St George Bank. I was speaking to a young woman who used to work in our home loans division, and is now a brand manager at St George. She told me Gail Kelly really inspired her. I asked her how, and one of the things she said was: 'She does these group voicemails once a month. She lets us all know what's happening and what she's thinking and what challenges they're having. I really like that.'

Email and voicemail are fantastic because you can get a quick message to a lot of people in two minutes. But don't rely solely on it. Management by walking around is also vital. Get up and talk to people. Have a sandwich with them, have a coffee with them, pull up a chair next to their desk and ask how they're going. Have a chat in the corridor or in the elevator. All those things are really important.

Find out what inspires employees

Whenever I meet someone who's really inspired by the place they work, I always try to find out why. It might be the way their boss treats them, it might be the office culture or it may be a drive for continual improvement. Then see if you can incorporate that inspiring facet in your business. Keep asking questions to understand what excites people about their workplace.

Café communication

Our in-house café is a great communication hub for our team. They can build relationships and swap ideas with people from other areas of the business. I can be at a table with our office junior, a salesperson and someone from marketing, having a sandwich and chatting about all kinds of stuff, both business and non-business. It builds up great rapport. When I have lunch there I pick up so much useful feedback that I don't get in formal communication channels.

Quick and efficient meetings

Most meetings go too long. There's often a feeling that if you call a meeting it's got to go for a certain amount of time to have justified gathering six people into the room. Often everyone's time is wasted with a lot of waffle.

So I have a few simple rules to keep meetings quick and efficient:

- **Meetings should be as short as possible** — usually 15 to 30 minutes is sufficient.

- **The only people at the meeting are people that really need to be there** — far too many meetings include people who are on the edge of a project and don't really need to be there.

- **Always have an agenda** — if I don't have an agenda I will reschedule the meeting.

- **Get relevant information in advance** — if you think there's stuff that you'll need to read ahead of time, ask for it before the meeting.

- **Start on time** — if you have a meeting at 10.00 a.m. and only three of the four people are there, start with the three present and find out later why the fourth couldn't make it on time.

- **Start the meeting by trying to unearth any specific agendas that attendees have** — once everyone's had a chance to look at the agenda prepared before the meeting, I'll say 'What other issues do we need to handle at this meeting?' You get them upfront and I'll often put them on a whiteboard.

- **Remember, your goal is to make decisions** — that's the purpose of having the meeting. If you just need to inform the attendees about something say so. For example 'There's no decision to be made here, I just need to update you on what's happening in my division and how it's going to impact on you guys.'

- **Finish on time** — not as obvious as starting on time but just as important. If you have a meeting that goes from 10.00 a.m. to 11.00 a.m., and you haven't finished, postpone the balance of the agenda to another meeting. Otherwise you end up going forever and cutting into other meetings and appointments. It also makes people move faster to get everything done within that time.

- **Summarise the decisions that have been made** — have someone note action points and decisions and circulate them.

Chairing a meeting

If you're the meeting chairperson you have to find a balance between getting input and interactivity from the group, and making decisions and moving to the next issue. You can't be so dictatorial that people don't feel they've had the opportunity to have input. But you don't want discussions to ramble on forever.

The right balance often depends on the issues for discussion. The bigger the issue, the more time you may allow for discussion. But don't allow the meeting to get bogged down on the little things. Sometimes people argue for the sake of arguing. I'll often say, 'This issue's not really material to our business, so let's just decide. I hear what you've all said and here's what I'm going to decide to do — I'm going to agree with Barney, so let's head in that direction. If it doesn't work, Barney you come back to us and we'll review it in the future.'

How to find a business coach, accountant or consultant

Word of mouth is the best way to find a good business coach, accountant or consultant – in fact any professional service. With one email it's easy to get a dozen opinions from other businesspeople very quickly. Nowadays there's no excuse for anyone saying they're challenged getting referrals.

It's important to consider their track record, which is how I found my accountant and tax expert, Anthony Bell from Bell Partners. It's imperative that consultants quickly develop a good understanding of your business in order for you to obtain the best advice. Anthony's enthusiasm and commitment to providing the best service to our team are essential qualities in any consulting role.

7.

10 strategies to turbocharge your business

To give you an instant boost I've given you 10 strategies to turbocharge your business. They don't cost lots of money or need a long lead time to implement. They're all about changing your habits and attitudes. You can start using them right now. Don't even wait until you've finished reading this book — start today!

10 strategies to turbocharge your business

1. See more qualified customers face to face.

2. Send information in advance of meetings.

3. Expand your Rolodex.

4. Utilise technology.

5. Take more shots.

6. Get aligned.

7. The Positive Feedback Loop.

8. Don't let perfect get in the way of better.

9. The inspired profit mechanic.

10. The importance of continually re-inventing your business.

1. See more qualified customers face to face

Many years ago I had the pleasure of meeting one of the greats of the real estate world, Bob Bohlen from Brighton, Michigan. I met Bob at a conference in San Francisco. He gave a great speech with loads of incredible tips. But the one thing he said that really stuck in my mind was: 'The thing that sets me apart in the real estate world is the fact that every day I see five qualified customers, face to face.' It's a simple concept, but a very powerful way to accelerate your sales.

Who is a qualified customer? Someone who is actually in a position to do business with you right now — someone who's ready to buy. How do you know that? Before you meet any potential customers face to face, you or someone else must find out if they're ready to buy. Ask them several key questions to gauge their readiness.

When I had a potential property buyer on the phone I'd ask them, 'How many properties have you seen? How long have you been looking? You said you liked a property last month. Why didn't you buy that one? Have you got your finance ready?' I'd ask a series of about ten questions to qualify them, so I didn't waste my time driving someone around for hours that wasn't ready to buy.

If a customer wasn't qualified I'd help them to get qualified. For example, if someone hadn't organised finance yet I'd say, 'Before we start working together one of the most important things is that you get your finances ready, because the properties we handle sell quickly. We get the price right and the market's hot, so I don't want you to miss out by not being ready.' I'd then put them in touch with a good mortgage broker.

A lot of salespeople don't have this qualification process in place. They don't know what questions to ask or have the discipline to ask them. Work out the six to eight questions that will give you an indication about how ready to do business your customers are. Then ask them every time.

If you can see five customers a day who are qualified, that's going to have an enormous impact on your business, irrespective of your product. Why face to face? Because that's the best way to do business. It's probably the most time consuming, but it's certainly the most effective.

I had a really clear goal each day: to either get one offer accepted on a property, one contract exchanged or take one listing. And how would I do it? By seeing five qualified customers face to face every day.

2. Send information in advance of new business meetings

For most people in the world of sales it goes something like this:

A potential customer calls and requests a meeting to discuss your product or service. The salesperson puts the appointment in their diary. Finally, the salesperson sees the customer.

You can drastically improve your sales if you put in a little extra effort between scheduling the appointment and meeting the customer. After I received a sales enquiry, I was committed to sending that potential customer something that was meaningful, well presented and explained a little bit about my services, before I met them.

I knew there would be limited time and opportunity when we met, so I wanted to ensure that I arrived having already added value and assisted them to understand the sales process. In fact, I'd usually courier an information package within one hour. It would include testimonial letters from previous clients as well as useful information about buying or selling and our company.

Inevitably, when I arrived they were already predisposed to using my services because of this professional presentation.

Recently a company I was considering doing business with impressed me by sending a 12-slide PowerPoint presentation prior to our scheduled meeting, with case studies and previous successes. It established their credentials quickly and in a manner that worked for me. I didn't have time to read layers and layers of corporate guff. It was customised for us, mentioning issues relating specifically to my business, which set it apart from a generic presentation.

In the end our board decided on another company, however this company went from last on our shortlist to number two, simply because of that one little thing. And if the other group doesn't work out they're the only people we'll call.

3. Expand your Rolodex

While business often involves numbers, stock, inventory and the like, at the end of the day it's almost inevitably about people and relationships. The people you get to know, the way you treat them and the quality of your relationships with customers, employees and suppliers are all critical in building a business. Understand that business success is predominantly about relationships.

When I started selling real estate I knew nobody. I was 20 years old and only three years out of school. I had no networks or relationships other than a few close friends and some football buddies. I set out each day to meet at least one new person, looking to sow the seeds of a future relationship.

I didn't have access to a computer database so I'd put their details on a 3" x 5" card system. I'd record their contact details, information about them and their family, hobbies and anything that would help me recall them when we next met.

Over the years these relationships would build and people would introduce me to their friends and colleagues. Before long I had a fantastic network of people that I was doing business with, many of whom had become good friends.

Today I continue to enjoy many of the relationships I developed two decades ago. I feel that my network of friends and associates is not only my greatest asset but also one of the great rewards of my business.

Recognise that in business you need to create a positive experience with everyone you meet, to capture essential information about them, and then, with their permission, continue some form of communication. Some of this can be generic, people don't expect you to write them a personalised letter once a month, but you can send an interesting newsletter or e-bulletin from time to time.

Creating a contacts database

These days the two key contact details to capture are mobile phone number and email address. People are quite transient, so work and home numbers change all the time. Mobiles and email addresses are more likely to stay constant. To make your database more valuable you should also note anything that will allow you to personalise future communication. It could be the name of their spouse, where you met them, who referred you to them or their favourite sporting team. Ask yourself: 'What are some key pieces of information that could be relevant for my next communication with this person?'

4. Utilise technology

Technology allows you to do an increasingly greater volume of business. And yet some people are still doing business the way they did ten years ago. They were selling 10 units a month and now they might be doing 12. Improvements in technology should enable you to do five times the amount of business you were doing 10 years ago.

I can walk into my office, create an email and send it out to 5000 people, and in two minutes these 5000 people have a message, an offer or an opportunity from me, for very little outlay. So why wouldn't you use that technology? Take advantage of any available technology that will move your business forward.

I'm not very technologically minded. But I don't have to be to recognise a positive outcome from upgrading our technology. I don't need to know how our ad typesetting system works. All I need to know is that it saves us time and money, and allows us to offer better service to clients. It's just a matter of surrounding yourself with quality consultants or employees that can explain the basic outcomes. You don't need to know the details.

The digital camera dilemma

We resisted digital camera technology for a long time because we weren't convinced the quality would match traditional film-based photography. It's important for us to maintain a high standard of photographic reproduction. So even though there were monetary savings, we stayed with film because we wouldn't compromise on quality.

But a new supplier convinced us we didn't have to compromise quality. They did a series of shots with the latest equipment and compared them to our traditional photographers' work. The digital was significantly better. It was a win-win situation. Our costs were reduced and we have quicker turnaround times so our customers can get their homes on the market faster.

5. Take more shots

The legendary Canadian ice-hockey player Wayne Gretsky once said: 'You miss 100% of the shots you don't take.' His point was that you've got to get out there and take risks. Take plenty of shots and don't be too precious or selective about taking risks, because you never know which opportunities will prove to be the best and which will come to nothing.

I realised many years ago that all I could control was my actions, and what came from them was inevitably dependent on other things beyond my control. For example, I could certainly control the amount of calls I'd make when I was selling, but I couldn't control the response of the person on the other end of the line.

One of the things that I've done every day for the last 10 years is to go through the newspapers first thing in the morning to see what's happening. Never a day goes by that there's not something that represents a business opportunity. Often there's a story of a company that's growing rapidly or expanding interstate, or stories about people on the move. So I tear out these articles and send a message to the person or company.

One recent example was an email I sent to a guy who I had read was selling his company and looking to move overseas. I knew he had a beautiful waterfront home, so I sent him an email congratulating him on his company's sale and seeing if he was interested in selling his property. I didn't hear anything for some time, but I arrived at work one morning to find an email inviting me to meet him and look through his house. We ended up selling his house for more than $10 million. All from a three-line email I'd sent several months before.

6. Get aligned

If you have a team of 10 and they're all doing their own thing and not aligned to a common cause, it may not affect you that much next week. In fact, it probably won't affect you much next month. But by next year, your business will have suffered. In fact, without alignment to a common cause, it will start to slide backwards.

Does your business have a common cause? Does it have common ideals and goals such that everyone can bond together and say, 'We're really committed to these things. They're really important to us, so let's work together and set aside our egos and petty differences.'

The best things to get aligned with are a company mission and values that make people feel good. For me — and for a lot of our team — it's about creating something special and raising the bar for our industry. Not just improving the profit. Not just selling more property. But taking real estate to the next level. We all have this dream that one day the real estate world will focus on our office and say: 'Hang on — there's this little company down in Australia and they're doing some phenomenal stuff. They're innovative and really customer focused. We need to check this company out.'

We're excited and proud that people are starting to do that already. We're getting people dropping in from overseas saying,

'We've heard about your company, we'd love to have a look through your offices. Can we talk to you about how you're doing it?'

There's a sense of pride that goes with creating something that's better than the rest of the world. One of the greatest feelings I get is when one of my team says they're proud to say they work here. They go to a dinner party or barbecue and someone asks where they work — they say McGrath — and people say, 'Wow — that looks like a really cool business.' That makes them proud and it makes me proud.

7. The Positive Feedback Loop

How is it that some businesses achieve 10 times the results of other businesses in the same period of time? We know they don't work ten times harder. Average business owners already work twelve hours a day.

What happens is what I call the Positive Feedback Loop. It works like this: we do a really great job for a customer, they tell another customer who then lists their property with us. That gives us another signboard up in the marketplace and another opportunity to talk to twenty buyers who inquire about the property.

We treat those buyers very well and they go out and tell their friends and we get another listing, another signboard and another *sold* sign. Soon we've got several *sold* signs, so it's easy for us to recruit the top sales agent that works for one of our competitors, because she sees we are growing. When she comes on board she brings twenty customers with her. So now there are another four signboards and another three *sold* signs and so on. It just keeps building and building. Fast.

Once you get to the point of momentum, your business can grow faster and seemingly with less effort. Certainly with no more effort.

One of the things that often retards the growth of small business (and indeed big business too) is the limiting belief of many managers that to grow exponentially requires more capital and energy than they have. They don't even try to match the performance of icons of their sector because they believe (wrongly) that the climb up the mountain is too exhausting and too risky.

Your challenge is to harness the power of the Positive Feedback Loop and see how it can create incredible results in an amazingly short time space for you.

8. Don't let perfect get in the way of better

Success in business requires some basic elements to be well executed simultaneously: finance, production, management, administration, sales and marketing. Each of the basic elements is made up of a combination of smaller elements: business plans, products, advertisements, meetings, telephone calls, premises, etc.

What if you and your team decided to make each of these elements — both big and small — an art form? Imagine if you created an art form out of recruitment and talent management. And how about making an art form of creating a world-class company culture? What about the person responsible for making your business documents? Are they pleasing to the eye, well laid out, easy to complete, an art form in themselves? Or are they just boring old documents?

It's important to consider every element of your business as a work of art that you're constantly refining. But it's equally important to realise you've got to make do with what you've got right now. My point is that even though you're committed to improving every element of your business, you can't wait until they're perfect before you put them to use.

Making even a small change in order to get closer to perfect is better than saying, 'If I don't have the capacity to get something perfect right now, then I won't implement it.' Aim high and move towards your target one step at a time.

Anyway, the best way to improve your business elements is to take them for a test drive and get some mud on them. They might not be perfect yet, but you can head them in that direction by seeing how they perform in the real world and discovering what changes need to be made.

I'm a perfectionist, so I've had to control my inclination to wait until everything is perfect on a project before I put it into action. As a friend once said, 'If you waited for every traffic light to turn green you'd never leave the driveway'.

If I was updating our website I'd want to wait until every function, every font and every feature was exactly spot on before releasing it to the public. But one of the things I've learnt from the IT world is you just get your site up there, then set about finetuning it. That way, people are using the site and giving feedback — and feedback is the best way to improve your business.

This of course doesn't mean you can throw substandard material into the marketplace. There has to be a sensible middle ground. I'd say, 'OK, we're building a new website. Let's give ourselves 30 days to get the prototype up. It won't be perfect, but let's get it up there. We'll put a feedback button on it, and ask our family and friends to visit the site. Every thirty days we'll evolve it to a new level.' In twelve months you can guarantee it will be a high quality website.

Many people resist change within an organisation. But you have to create a company culture that is comfortable with change. Everyone has to agree that to get from here to where you want to be, some significant changes will be made along the way.

Sometimes you have to overcome people's natural resistance to change. Whenever there's any hesitation about an innovation or a new initiative we're embarking upon, we trial it for 90 days. If within that time it's not operating effectively, or the team and/or the customers don't like it, we whip it out of the marketplace. How much damage can you do in 90 days?

If you place a framework around a change, people are less inclined to feel locked in. 90 days gives people time to get accustomed to the change, to provide feedback, and to improve the new initiative. And in 13 years of business we have rarely taken anything out of the market.

The team actually enjoys this trial system — staff surveys tell us that people love the constant change within our company. Seven or eight years ago people felt things were changing too much. But we've changed the culture since then, and now people look forward to the next innovation rather than being fearful of what change may bring.

9. The inspired profit mechanic

For the first four or five years after I started my business I didn't make a profit. I went through a stage of having second thoughts, wondering, 'Have I done the right thing? Maybe I should have stayed an employee? I was making a lot more money then.'

After some time I realised I had focused solely on building a business and not on making steady profits. All I wanted to do was sell more property, delight more customers, get more sales and get more sold signs up. Not that this is a bad thing. But I also needed to focus on creating a business that cranks out profit as well.

Profit wasn't where my head was at. My head was purely growth. Many business owners with great business plans, great people and great intent, still go broke. Because they're not profit mechanics. They're not structuring their business to create profits along the way. Your goal should always be to create a profitable, sustainable business, not just a great business. Not just a customer-focused business, but a profitable customer-focused business.

Statistics say that 90% of small businesses fail within five years. Why do they fail? Simply because they didn't make a profit. It's reasonable to assume many of those failed businesses were great businesses. They were providing great customer service. They had great customer focus, probably great people. But they just didn't make it to the point of profitability. So it's really important to focus not only on a killer business plan, hiring wonderful staff, developing innovative marketing and improving your product, but also on maximising profit.

10. The importance of continually re-inventing your business

To be successful in business requires constant review — to make sure you stay on track — and constant re-invention to improve performance. You have to look at what's working and what's not working. My business coach talks about start, stop, continue. What do you have to start doing? What do you have to stop doing? What do you have to continue doing?

You need to regularly review yourself and your business. What must this business stop doing that it's been doing this year? Is it inconsistent service delivery? Is it poor recruiting? Did we make 10 out of 12 average recruits this year? Therefore, let's review our recruitment process. Let's read a book on great recruitment. Let's ask different questions when we're recruiting.

Are the premises getting tatty? Are they getting tired? The website, the training and development program, the financial structure? All those things; just have a good look at them and ask yourself those questions about what you have do.

Incremental improvement is important, but remember: it's thinking outside the box that can lead to quantum leaps in business. You have to be continually on the lookout for ways to re-invent the business. It could be new technology, an additional service element, a new business unit, or a new role that you create within your business.

Let me give you an example:

TWA, the US airline, invented business class in the '70s. Their marketing manager believed business passengers who needed to work on flights would pay more to have more space in their seats. So they trialled a new section in the aeroplane. Business class: more roomy than economy, but less expensive than first class.

Virtually every other major airline dismissed the idea, saying it wouldn't work — people will either pay to have huge seats and deluxe service up the front or want a cheap ticket down the back. But it did work. TWA stole a big lead on their competition and grabbed a huge market share.

I refer to these total business re-invention ideas as my 'TWAs'. These are the ideas that would not just improve how we're going, but totally revolutionise the business. You have to be constantly finetuning the business all the time. But don't forget to keep an eye out for your TWAs.

Regular meetings with your key people

I got a great idea about morning meetings with my executive team from Rudi Giuliani's book *Leadership*. He would get his key team together first thing in the morning and run through the day's events, what was expected and what happened yesterday. So I decided to trial it. I put it to my executive team and they were keen to give it a go, so we did.

We meet several mornings a week at 9.00 a.m. We have a loose agenda. Basically, we talk about what's happening in each person's day and what happened yesterday. Is there anything we can support each other with? Any challenges? Any great wins in the business that I can send an email about or go and say congratulations to someone?

It's been a fantastic initiative for us. It's helped improve the culture and it's increased our respect and understanding for what each of us is doing. The cross-support within the executive level and right through the business has been enhanced dramatically from this one simple idea.

PART THREE

You+leadership

8.

Leaders get the team they deserve

Many businesspeople don't realise that the results on the balance sheet at the end of the year are intrinsically linked to the quality and performance of management and leadership in the business. To be successful in business it's essential to develop good leadership qualities and management habits. If you get this right, many other things will simply fall into place.

If you're not happy with your team it's important to take responsibility for the situation. Ask yourself what you can do to improve it. 'Maybe I'm not attracting or keeping the best people because of my leadership skills — or lack of leadership skills.' That's a really powerful position to start from, because if you work on getting your team operating well, your whole business will be transformed.

Energy starts at the top

Mahatma Gandhi once said: 'We must become the change we want to see.' And that's how it is with leadership. If you want a team that's excited, passionate, motivated and energised, that's exactly how you've got to be. Culture is caught not taught — if your leaders are energised and excited, their positive energy will be passed on to all the team members. Before you know it you'll have a highly energised organisation.

First of all, you've got to be operating at a high level of energy yourself. If you're out of shape, physically sluggish and only operating at 50% energy, you're not going to have a company that's operating at 100%.

It's also a good idea to share your excitement with all your staff. Once a month we get everyone together and I tell my team what I'm really excited about. I'll talk about it in a very passionate way. I'll reinforce our vision of where the business is going. I'll describe all the exciting aspects of it. I let that excitement ripple through the whole team. If a leader gets excited, the team is going to get excited!

Keep it open

We have an open plan office where every executive, manager and employee has the same size desk. I have found this working environment has many benefits:

1. Management can easily pick up on the energy of the team and pump it up if necessary.

2. Communication is freer and easier.

3. Business owners and managers are more accessible to the team for sharing information and giving support.

4. It facilitates 'management by walking around'.

5. It promotes egalitarianism.

6. An open plan layout is more cost effective.

Company mission and values

If you could define in a sentence what you want your company to do, achieve or be, that's a company mission. Whatever it is your business is destined to do becomes your company's mission statement.

Being clear about your company mission helps you stay in touch with the big picture. By reminding you what you're trying to achieve it guides you in decision-making. You can evaluate your choices based on how they will move you closer to achieving your mission.

If your company mission is what you're trying to achieve, your company values reflect how you intend to carry out your mission. Company values are the principles and standards that you deem most important to the business, such as honesty, openness, passion, innovation or efficiency. They mould the personality of your organisation and guide its behaviour in the marketplace.

One of our key values is integrity, because we know that without it we have nothing. We only have one reputation and if we blow it we're finished. Humility is really important for us. We know that one of the dark sides of success is arrogance. So we're really committed to keeping our feet on the ground.

We're also very big on community. We're part of a community that gives us great support and provides us with tremendous business opportunities. If we don't contribute back to the community, the karmic loop is broken and our success will be short-lived.

It doesn't matter what business activity you're doing, the common theme must always be your values. So everything we do, we do with integrity and humility, and with regard to what's best for the community.

We make our company values clear to new employees from day one. All our new recruits have an induction day (two days for salespeople) and I give the opening talk. Company values are the first thing I talk about.

But we don't expect our new employees to be ingrained with our values after only one induction session. We continue to reinforce our values through workshops where we demonstrate how they can be applied in the real world.

For example, we might workshop with our team how our values come into play when tenants are signing a new lease. How do you negotiate with openness and honesty? Do you just hand them the lease and a pen, or do you make sure that you explain every single potential thing that could ever cause an issue with the tenants?

Are you humble? Do you put the customers' interests first, listen to what they have to say, and share in their enthusiasm and excitement? Do you show up on time? Because the opposite of humility is arrogance, and arrogance is when you think your time is more important than your customers'.

We reiterate our company values constantly. We do it at our monthly team meetings, in between team meetings, at presentations, during one-on-one counselling and in performance feedback sessions. It's a really important part of our culture and we want everyone coming on board and everyone that's on the team to know how important it is.

Change happens every single day, but the values of the organisation should be constant.

Manage by exception

Trust and self-management are central to our company culture, so we believe in managing by exception. We're not out there looking for people doing the wrong thing. Once we've let the team know what's expected of them, we trust them to do the right thing. But if we find out through a complaint, customer feedback or by observation that someone's off course, we deal with it immediately, openly and fairly.

Clarity on roles and responsibilities

Everyone on your team has to be clear about their roles and responsibilities. Not just what tasks they must perform in their job, but what role they can play in the great success of your business.

The job description is a good place to start — these are the 10 things we expect you to do brilliantly. But it's important to get staff thinking beyond their daily work tasks to 'How else can I add value to this business?'

These 'extracurricular' responsibilities are no less important than what's on their job description and are an important part of building a world-class culture. They're things like contributing at team meetings, wildly applauding when one of their colleagues gets an award, and celebrating others' success when they're a little bit too shy or humble to share it.

We let everyone know that even though their business card may not say 'leader' or 'ambassador', we expect them to be both. We encourage every employee to be a leader within the business, to give support to their colleagues and set a good example, and to be an ambassador for the company when they step outside the office.

The scourge of us versus them

When arrogance, materialism or inequality infiltrate management the result is usually discord. An 'us versus them' mentality can lead to feelings of distrust and bitterness between management and staff. It's divisive and destructive, and not at all conducive to operating at maximum efficiency. The antidote to this scourge is transparency and egalitarianism.

We have set up a totally transparent organisation. Every month we talk to our team about the numbers we're doing. We tell them when we're on budget, below budget, above budget, what's working, what's not working and the challenges the business is facing. We tell the team exactly how it is and how we're doing — we don't hide anything.

There are no 'corner offices' at McGrath. All our managers sit out in an open plan environment with the rest of the team. No-one has an office — everyone sits at a one-metre wide workspace. All of our meeting rooms have glass walls so everyone can see what's happening inside.

Anyone can come by at any time, sit down and chat to me. They don't need an appointment. The same applies for all the other members of the management team. I'm a big believer in management by walking around. I visit our regional offices every week just to see the team. Sometimes I just sit in an office with no set tasks. I know people will come up and tell me what's going right and what's going wrong, and it's critical for me to listen to their feelings and views.

Minimise office politics

In any business there's always going to be some office politics. There'll be some degree of envy, one-upmanship, hidden agendas and personality clashes. Don't panic about it – it's a part of life. You need to control it to a point where it's not going to cause you problems. But don't be so naive as to think you can eliminate it entirely. You've just got to minimise the politics so it becomes a minor inconvenience, rather than a major disruption.

Don't change for me

A friend of mine recently spent some time in the office with me. She's a keen observer and a student of business, and as we walked around the office she was taking it all in. Later she told me, 'John, it's really cool that when you walk around the office, people don't flinch, they don't change what they're doing, they don't change who they are. They just keep doing what they're doing.'

She said that in her view it was a really positive sign for the organisation that people weren't intimidated by me, they weren't scared, they didn't change who they were around me. I'd never noticed that, but I was really thrilled she'd made that observation. It endorsed what we are doing as a company, the values we try to adhere to, and the culture we're working to create.

9.

Building a world-class culture - and keeping it

Your culture is a fundamental way to differentiate your business from your competitors and lay the foundations for long-term profits. Conversely, a frail or fractured company culture can send even the best product into oblivion. Many company cultures just evolve over time by default, for better or worse. But by consciously creating an energised and customer-focused culture you're in the driver's seat for success.

In essence, culture is the energy put out by a company. It's the thought process that pervades most of the team most of the time. It's what you feel when you walk into a company or store or what you hear when you call on the phone. It's the personality of a company. So there's no doubt that it's important to get it right and keep it right.

But one observation before we start on culture. In many companies there are multiple cultures. In fact typically there can be as many cultures in one company as there are divisions or managers. So as you look within you might need to address a multicultural organisation just like a community with different groups within it.

To find out how you create a world-class culture and capture the same sort of spirit engendered by some of the great start-up companies like Apple in the '70s or Netscape in the '90s, read on.

Leaders create the buzz

In my experience, the one thing that sets great companies apart from merely average ones is their buzz: the invisible energy that flows through their corporate veins.

It's how you feel when you speak to the receptionist or walk into the showroom. It's the vibe at the sales meetings and in the work areas. It's the enthusiasm you get from an employee you bump into at a function when you ask where they work. It's the sparkle in the eyes of the people who work there.

Maintaining the buzz is one of the major roles I have in my company. How do I do it? There's no manual or set of instructions, but I'll give you a few examples of little things I do and you'll get a sense of how it might work for you.

When I'm at work I make sure I'm in the best frame of mind I can be. I always lead by example with a happy and positive attitude. And fortunately I don't need to fake it because I love what I do and the people I work with! But I am very aware of how important it is to be excited and positive every day.

My assistant once observed that despite the fact we now have six offices and over 280 people on our team, when I'm distracted or in a bad mood she senses a loss of energy throughout the company. Now I'm not sure how accurate that is, but even if there's an ounce of truth in it, it's an expensive and self-defeating exercise for a leader to have too many 'bad days' at work.

I really make the effort to get to know each and every member of my team. Not only does this help build rapport, but I can also keep close to how they're performing energetically. Are they excited about what they're doing? Is their career developing? Do they have any issues outside of work that we can support them through?

It's not hard to ascertain these things. I do it by speaking to my management team weekly about their people. Is there anyone we need to give some extra attention or support? Is there a team member they feel might need some inspiration or encouragement?

I leverage the closer relationships my managers have with their team to see how I can support individual team members. Support can come in different forms, from a quick chat at their desk, an encouraging email, perhaps even a call to their spouse or parents.

I've often called the parents of my junior team members to say hi and tell them how well their son or daughter is doing. They get a blast from hearing such positive reports and it builds an important bridge between our company and our extended family.

One of my favourite roles is to check in on the teams in each of our different offices. I sometimes get a bag of hot cinnamon donuts and a tray of cappuccinos and just arrive unannounced. It's a great way of breaking the team's normal day-to-day routine and gives them a mental break. Plus I love donuts, so that's an added bonus for me!

Body language

One of the best ways to assess someone's energy is by observing their body language. No matter how hard people may try to mask their true feelings or energy, it's almost impossible to fake your body language. By watching their posture, eye contact (or lack of it), interaction with others, tone of voice and facial expressions, you quickly can tell who's in great shape and who's feeling challenged.

Aligned is the key

In order to develop a great culture you must ensure there's alignment amongst the key people — partners, managers and stakeholders. Companies with great cultures inevitably have a common vision and set of goals that everyone is aligned with. They constantly seek to eradicate hidden agendas and don't entertain politics.

Alignment is best achieved by constant communication throughout the company. The days of employees being told only what they 'need to know' are long gone. Enlightened organisations tell their team everything about the company. This creates a sense of ownership within the team as well as providing transparency.

Improving culture the hard way

When my business was only a few years old, two of my salespeople came into my office. Not only were they my best sales-

Small business can change on a dime

The smaller the business is, the faster it can change. If you're a one-person business, you can change real fast just by making new decisions. If you've got a business of 10, it doesn't take long to get everyone committed to a new vision. If you've got a business of 2000, it's going to take a little more time.

people, but they were my great friends at the time. They sat down and I immediately sensed there was a problem. They looked uncomfortable. In fact they looked decidedly sick. 'We've decided to leave the company,' one of them said. Ouch! That was a hard thing to hear for the first time when you're growing your dream. But the worst was yet to come: they'd decided to join our number one competitor. Double-whammy!

It's hard enough to lose a great team member. Let alone a friend. Let alone two of them simultaneously. And then have them cross the street to our competitor. It was extremely hard for me to take. Financially. Personally. In every way.

But I quickly realised that feeling sorry for myself wasn't going to benefit me or the business. So I looked for the gift. What possibly could come out of this that could benefit me?

I thought to myself, 'Why would someone want to leave here? We're offering a great environment, fantastic career opportunities and excellent facilities.' Or so I thought.

About three months later I asked one of them why they left. I gotta tell you it's painful to have someone tell you why they don't love you (and your company) any more. But you need to hear it if you're to move up to the next level. Once I learned why they didn't see our company as the best place to be any more I was able to set about changing it for the better.

There were only a few things that needed changing. In fact that's been my experience — a few small tweaks can make a world of difference to your culture. So I methodically set about finetuning, adjusting, and polishing all the areas of the business that had gathered cobwebs or lost some focus. The end result was a much-improved business, a better place to work, more profitable for shareholders and a much stronger platform from which to grow the business.

The moral of the story? Don't wait until your employees bail out to find out what they don't like about your culture. (Later I'll explain how you can make sure your employees tell you exactly what they think of you.)

Giving recognition

When a manager or business owner gives a staff member recognition for a job well done it creates a jolt of positive energy that runs through the entire company. Recognition can be face to face, it can be through a team leader, or it can be in a voicemail. Whichever way you send it, you just gotta give people recognition.

I once got a fantastic email from a client praising one of our staff. It was the best feedback email I'd ever received. I immediately responded to the client telling them that it was one of the most positive emails I'd received in 15 years, and I cc'd the staff member's managers. I printed the email and walked around to her office to give her the good news.

I made it into a little celebration. I told her how proud and excited I was that her work generated this sort of feedback. There are so many moments of recognition like this if you look out for them. And every one gives the whole organisation a little lift.

We also have regular awards such as team member of the month. All the employees and managers nominate one of their colleagues and we choose the best one. Then I invite them in front of the team and get their manager to tell everybody why this person has been awarded team member of the month. Then I'll add on top of that any observations I've had. And then I'll say 'Has anyone else had this experience from this person?' You make them feel like a hero. That creates incredible energy every month.

Catch people doing things right

Be positive. Look for ways of catching staff doing things right and reward them, rather than trying to catch them doing something wrong.

Mentoring

Mentoring is a great way to introduce the business culture to new team members. It also gives new recruits someone they can go to for guidance and counsel about any areas of the job or organisation that they're unsure about or having difficulty with.

We have a buddy system where every new recruit is appointed a buddy who becomes their de facto mentor. It's usually a peer from another department within the organisation. The buddy helps introduce our company culture and supports them with practical guidance and advice. They can discuss any concerns, issues or challenges they might be experiencing with their buddy.

There's no fixed time period for this arrangement. It continues for as long as it needs to, and the buddies invariably end up good friends. The buddy system has worked very well for us, both helping to integrate new employees into the business and fostering an environment of mutual support.

We also have a Future Leaders group, which is a more structured mentoring program for 10 of our junior staff who have management potential. We have monthly sessions with them, and talk through leadership concepts. We go into a little more detail about the business strategy, what's going well and what's not going so well.

Each month we give them a business book to read. We debrief each month's book and talk about what they learned and how that could be applied to our business. We brainstorm specific issues and get their feedback on how they feel the business is going and how we could do it better.

The main benefit of mentoring is having the support of someone who is understanding, interested and caring, and can offer an objective perspective. It doesn't have to be a professional business coach, although you can use them as well. Often your thoughts get jumbled up in your head and it's hard to find some clarity. Having a conversation with a caring listener is a great way to organise and assess your thoughts and then work out your priorities.

Leading from the heart

Great business leaders are now looking beyond spreadsheets and business plans for guidance on how to run their operations. They realise their intellect can only get them so far and that there's a more powerful source of inspiration and wisdom that they can tap into — their hearts.

Each of us has an incredible internal wisdom and consciousness which we can use to guide us in the marketplace. Think of it as the wise tribal elder within you. Someone who's tapped into the shared consciousness and always knows the right thing to do. I encourage people to get in touch with that part of themselves.

You'll still need to use your head for business problem solving. But also let your heart play a role in the development of the business. I don't run my business purely on one or the other, but I'd say 90% of my decisions are ultimately made by what's in my heart as opposed to what's in my head. Head is good. Heart is great. Head and heart together are unbeatable.

It's all about trust

Being in your heart is a lot about trust. You have to trust yourself, and you have to trust your team members. We've all got the answers within, we just rarely trust ourselves. Yet our heart is the best guidance system on the planet. Just ask yourself the simple question: 'Does this feel right?'

Some people call it intuition or a gut feeling. It's that feeling of knowingness or comfort or discomfort around decisions and situations. When you walk into something and you know it's not right, you can sense it in your body. We all have it — you just have to learn how to tap into it.

I'll give you an example. One year, just before Christmas, the landlord of our Leichhardt office announced he was raising the rent five per cent. 'But the market hasn't gone up,' we said (in fact we felt it had gone down). 'Bad luck. The lease says that at this particular time we can put it up five per cent, so we're going to do it,' he replied. Even though we could afford the extra money, we told the landlord we'd look around.

My Chief Operating Officer came to me and asked if we just wanted to pay the extra five per cent, but I said, 'I don't feel right about it.' He said, 'Well, they can give us a month's notice and we've got a staff of 30 over there.' It was a difficult situation. But rather than go into panic mode I said to myself, 'This was meant to happen. The landlord was meant to play hard ball and was meant to throw us out on Christmas Eve, because there's a better opportunity waiting for us.' I told him, 'Don't worry, we'll find a better place.'

Two days later he came in to see me and said, 'A board's just gone up on a great property down the street. It's exactly what we're looking for. It's less rent, it's bigger, it gives us room to expand.' I drove over there the next day and saw it was perfect. I called up the agent and arranged to sign the new lease. Our new landlord was so excited about us moving into his premises he wanted to create a little ceremony when we signed the lease. He wanted to personally hand deliver the keys and have us over for dinner with his family.

So by going with our feelings and following our hearts we'd gone from a dire situation of having a landlord who wanted to screw us on a technicality to having a great new premises and a landlord who wanted to celebrate having us in his building. It was a totally different energy.

5.

Recruiting your world-class team

Are good people hard to find? Is there a shortage? You'd always love to have more of them, and it would be great if they were easier to come by. But the reality is that you'll find as many good people as you deserve. You can't change the quality of people out on the street looking for a job, but you can change your ability to attract and keep the right ones.

There are a lot of business owners who say 'Oh I can't get any good people' or 'Good people don't stay around, they want to take off and do their own thing.' But there are many great organisations around the world that attract and retain great people.

We're fortunate to get 20 to 30 work enquiries by email a week, because we've developed a reputation and created a culture that people seem to aspire to. But no matter whether people come knocking on your door or you have to go out to find them, there are a few ways of ensuring you make the best quality recruitments.

What I look for in a potential employee

The essential traits that I look for in all potential employees are as follows:

- **Passion** — you can teach product knowledge and you can teach sales skills, but it's impossible to teach passion. You've either got the excitement, enthusiasm and energy or you ain't.

- **Determination** — in a sales and customer service environment and in any business that's growing fast, there are always going to be some difficult challenges. You need people that are determined to get through them.

- **Flexibility** — an ability to adapt to change rather than resist it. We're definitely an organisation of change. The way we do things this year could be radically different to the way we do them next year. So it's really important to find people who are naturally adaptable.

- **Ambition** — we don't allow arrogance, but we still want ambition. We want people that want to get ahead, and we know the smart ones will realise the way to get ahead is by providing great service and developing their skills.

- **Balance** — we want people who are prepared to work hard, but we realise there's much more to life than just work. Everyone has their own life path, whether it's to build a family or follow other passions outside work. You can still follow your path and work for us. I find people who have a full life outside work are more interesting and better at serving our customers than people who have real estate tunnel vision.

- **Integrity** — life's too short to deal with people that don't have integrity. A stellar real estate sales record means nothing without integrity. I don't care if we could boost our bottom line by millions of dollars a year — I'd rather wait and get the right person with integrity than to take on a successful salesperson that doesn't have integrity.

- **Clarity** — people who know where they're going, what they want and what they expect. If I ask, 'Where do you see yourself in five years?' I really appreciate it if someone can articulate a plan they've drawn up for themselves.

- **Responsibility** — you don't want to have to hold people's hands 24/7. So you need people who are able to manage themselves. But more than that, you need people who can take total responsibility and not blame others. You'll get clues to this by asking why they're leaving their current position. If they start blaming their boss, co-workers or anything else, you know they're not taking responsibility for themselves.

- **Personality** — not any one particular type of personality, just a pleasing disposition.

Attitude beats competency

When we're interviewing potential employees we look for attitude more than core competencies. Whether an administrative person types at 50 words a minute or 90 words a minute is rarely of huge interest to us, so long as they can type at a reasonable speed, that's okay. What's important is if they're passionate about working for this organisation, that they're humble, not arrogant, and that they're totally honest with us.

What I look for in a CV

Essentially, a CV is a sales document. So the most important aspect for me is the presentation. If it's well laid out, easy to understand, with high attention to detail, easy to assimilate the information and shows some personality, I'm impressed. If not, then God help you on a sales presentation!

I rarely read the minute details. I receive hundreds of CVs and I don't think I've ever read one front to back.

I like people who cut to the core with no unnecessary detail or clutter. So the perfect CV on my desk would be a beautifully laid out one-pager that briefly summarises their previous work history, talks about their future aspirations, describes who they are in real terms as a person, and outlines their strengths and what areas they're working on.

Throw away the CV

When you're interviewing new staff throw away their CVs and look into their eyes and hearts and say to yourself, 'Is this person passionate about doing great work?' Look for that spark that says they want to make a difference. That's what's most important.

What to ask candidates in a job interview

A lot of managers don't ask candidates the right questions in interviews, so they just get standard answers. Most candidates can pre-empt what they're going to be asked. Before the interview they'll prepare their lines like an actor in a movie. So what you've got to do is ask questions they don't expect. Ask them about their life plans and passions and try to tap into their real self.

Get away from the traditional recruitment talk, going through their resume and asking the candidate to tell you a bit about themselves. Try to get to the essence of who someone really is, rather than who they want you to think they are.

I'll often ask someone, 'What are you not good at?' That's often one of the most telling things about a person. I respect people who know the areas they need to improve on. I'm very wary of people who have never thought about it.

None of us are perfect and hopefully all of us are working to improve something in our lives right now. So I might say, 'Tell me about a project or situation where you encountered a challenge that required a major shift in thinking.' I'm looking for anecdotal evidence of how they've handled the challenges life has handed them, and what their thinking process was.

People can compile a highly polished presentation, but that doesn't mean they're right for your business. I've often dropped in on people at their home — especially if it's a senior appointment. I'll try to meet them when they're off guard, because you see a different energy when someone isn't expecting you. You have to look for the little signals about people that you might not see when they step into your foyer in a three-piece suit.

Our HR manager does the first line of interviews with anyone coming to work with us. Then they meet the leader of the team they'd be joining. Lastly, in many instances, I'll interview them.

They're told that I'm going to interview them and the interview will rarely last more than five minutes. I don't want them to have expectations that they're going to be here for an hour. They might be offended, but that's as long as it takes me. I rely heavily on my intuition. I look someone in the eyes, chat for a few minutes, and I'll get a feeling. Often I can tell by watching how someone sits in reception if they're going to be the right person.

Smart questions to evaluate job candidates

- Tell me of a successful project you managed from start to finish and how you did it?
- How do you work under pressure with deadlines?
- How do you define working too hard?
- How do you manage stress in your life?
- What would be several things you would do in your first 30 days of working for our company in this position?
- What role do you typically play in a team environment?
- What are your weaknesses?
- Persuade me to move to your suburb?
- What work are you most proud of?
- How have you changed in the last 12 months – where have you developed most?
- What's most important to you about your career and this position?
- What sort of leadership style do you thrive under?

People join companies, but leave leaders

Generally people want to work with an organisation because of its reputation. They go through the interview process and, if successful, arrive in the organisation hoping they've landed their dream job. But if somewhere down the track they're not getting personally fulfilled, they don't find the environment inspiring, or they're not given the tools they need to do a great job every day, they'll become dissatisfied and start looking elsewhere.

Employees want the opportunity to move their career to new levels. For that to happen certain conditions need to be present in the organisation. And the person who can create these conditions is the leader. So if employees aren't hanging around, it's probably because their leader isn't able to meet their needs.

Team members don't get out of bed in the morning and come to work to be mediocre. Yet staff everywhere are under-performing. So where's the disconnect? It's because they haven't been given the opportunity; they haven't been inspired by someone to go to the next level. It all comes back to leadership.

11.

Leading (and keeping) your world-class team

A business never outpaces its leader. The success or failure of a business usually comes down to the behaviour of an individual or a small group, because the culture of the business arises from the habits of the leadership.

So if you want your business to grow, you've got to grow. It's that simple. If you keep evolving as a leader, the business will go with you automatically. And you can start right now by implementing some of these essential skills for leading your business to prosperity.

Getting to know your people

One of my most enjoyable roles as CEO is 'management by walking around'. I picked up this idea years ago in Tom Peters' book *In Search of Excellence*. He said that managers needed to come down from their ivory towers and be with their most important constituents: their staff.

At first this was easy because the entire team sat in the same room for the first two years. It was easy to get to know everyone, give support and communicate important issues. Those were the days of 'real time reporting' because every phone call was overheard by at least half the staff, so there were no secrets!

Nowadays our company has grown to over 300 staff in six regional offices. I spend at least two days a week just roaming around the company, feeling the pulse, getting to know new team members and making sure anyone who wants to tell me something has the opportunity to do so face to face.

Ideas flow up

One of the major benefits of having an egalitarian culture is that it facilitates communication through all levels. Many of our ideas come from the team up, not the management down. It indicates that our team is thinking about innovation and they're thinking about how they can create a better environment for themselves and for our customers. It's also a sign that they're comfortable communicating their ideas to management and that's a very positive situation.

Talent management

'We're all in the talent management business.' MARTIN SORRELL

If you're a manager or business owner, 90% of your role is talent management. Because 90% of your challenges and issues are going to come from your people, and 90% of your wins, successes and business growth will come from your people.

Technology enables you to do business and marketing can get the phones ringing. But at the end of the day, it's the calibre of your people that will have the biggest impact on moving your business forward.

If you were the CEO of the LA Lakers basketball team, what would your focus be? It's likely that you'd put most of your effort into assembling the best team and keeping them on board. Well guess what? It's the same thing for business.

We've got three key groups we focus on in our business. In order of priority they are:

1. Our people
2. Our customers
3. Our shareholders

I don't sit in my office all day contemplating how I can make the shareholders of this business more money. (I figure that's a natural by-product of looking after our staff.) And while we have a very customer-centric business, I don't just sit there saying, 'What is it I can do today for the customer?'

Engage your people

'Numbers are the end result. You change a business by changing the behaviour of its people.'
DICK BROWN, CHAIRMAN AND CEO OF EDS

I've never seen a business plan that hasn't made an enormous profit on the Excel spreadsheet, yet most businesses struggle or go broke. Success isn't predominantly about the plan, the data, the available technology or even the finance.

It's about engaging your people, getting them performing at the right level and getting them excited about what they're doing. Do they love their customers? Are they aligned with the company's plan? Do they understand their role in contributing to the outstanding performance of the business? Are they happy and excited? If you want your business to do better, change the behaviour of your people.

What I mostly think about is, how can we empower our team? How can we get them more excited? How can we get them more focused? How can we get them delivering more to our customers? Of course you've also got to pay attention to the bottom line and your customers. But first and foremost you should concentrate on talent management.

By focusing your attention and energy on developing your staff you create a domino effect. If you look after your people they'll naturally look after your customers. If you look after your customers then the profit will look pretty healthy at year end.

Fulfilment = retention

The days of a career for life are long past. Now it's more like 'a career until I'm not happy in this position anymore'. The workforce is increasingly mobile, so staff retention is a big issue for most businesses.

The best way to keep your team on board is to enable them to improve their skills and live up to their potential. People rarely leave their job for financial reasons. The majority of people leave because they're not fulfilled and not having fun.

A lot of small businesspeople that I talk to have a scarcity mentality around staff development. Their attitude is, 'I don't want to train my staff up, because then they'll just leave and I will have wasted my money and effort.' So they end up with their team performing below par, and then cross their fingers and hope their staff will stick around.

So you have a choice: train and develop your people and they might leave. Or, don't train and develop them and they might stay, which is far scarier!

Our experience has been that if you develop people, encourage them, support them, coach them, give them new skills, give them scope to improve and show them how their role makes a difference to the entire business, then they're likely to stay and be a productive contributor to the business.

A learning environment

One thing we hope to get across at our new staff interviews is that we're a learning organisation. I say to new staff members, 'If you're a real learner and you love new information, this is the greatest company on the planet. But if you think you're at a stage where you've learnt enough, we have a problem. You're going to hate it.'

We set up an expectation with our team that we want them to learn as much as possible while they're with us, and we hope that's forever. But if it's not, we still want them to learn as much as possible. Learning is a really big part of our culture and it takes place on a formal and informal basis.

We have an extensive business and self-development library so staff can borrow audio tapes and books. If I find an interesting article on the Web I'll email the link around to the team and encourage them to check it out.

Our sales teams have regular Friday morning training sessions where we get our top agents to talk through what's working for them with the rest of the team. Then there's a Q and A session when newer agents can pick the old hands' brains about how they'd handle particular situations, or what helped them to get started in their careers.

We also have regular information forums with other teams within the organisation. We have our Future Leaders group where we encourage the development of some of our younger staff members who have shown potential. We have a women's group for our female staff.

All these hubs of information create a ripple effect throughout the entire business. I'd estimate that 75% of the education and information sharing in our organisation is peer to peer. So for example, if I give my leadership team some tips and information in a coaching session, and they then go and share this with their team, the information spreads by osmosis.

We're really a business that's learning. We've created a culture where people not only expect to learn, but they actually look forward to the next coaching session or useful piece of information in their inbox.

Success Inventory Checklist

A few years ago I gave a talk to a small business group. Phil Gould, who coaches the Sydney City Roosters rugby league team, was on before me, and I sat in the audience and listened to his talk before I went on.

Gould has coached the Australian and NSW representative sides and he's one of the greatest football coaches ever in Australia, in my opinion, with a high success record. He talked about some of the tactics he uses to get the top performance from his team. He gave me a great idea for improving my team's performance.

At the beginning of each season, Gould gets everyone in his squad of 30 players to fill out an incredibly detailed self-assessment on their skills. Doing a self-assessment isn't such an earth-shattering idea, but what caught my attention was the detail he went into.

Some coaches might just ask their players to rate themselves on the basics: 'What's your defensive game like? Your offensive game? How's your strategy? Fitness?' But Gould got his players to really delve into the tiny details of their game.

He asked: 'What are you like passing on your left hand side? Your right hand side? What are you like with long passes? Short passes? What are you like mentally preparing for a home game? An away game? What's your diet like during the week? What's your game day diet like?' And so on, for six pages. He made the players appraise themselves on very specific aspects to see where they needed to improve their performance.

I thought this was such a great idea, I decided to adapt it to our business. Because, for example, I knew it was important for real estate agents to have good product knowledge, but what exactly did that mean? So I broke it down and came up with nine specific aspects:

1. Architecture in your core area

2. Property values in your core area

3. History of your core area

4. Rental values in your core area

5. Sales contracts

6. Conveyancing processes

7. Finance and home loan options

8. Knowledge of other agents' listings in your core area at any given time

9. Knowledge of your key competitors' strengths and weaknesses

I went through all the key skills that a successful agent must possess (such as listing properties, negotiation, selling, vendor communication, etc) and broke them down into their detailed components. I put all these together on one survey which we called the McGrath Success Inventory Checklist. It runs to three pages with around 120 questions.

Each of our agents goes through the list and rates themselves from zero to 10 on each skill. Then their manager will go through it and make their assessment. The agent and their manager then get together and discuss the results. If the agent rates themselves only a four on selling auction listings above $1 million, then their manager can give them some coaching on that. If there's a big disparity between the agent's and manager's ratings, then they can discuss that and the manager can give some feedback.

We always get a tremendous response from the agents when they've done the Checklist. They say it helps them see all the little things that are letting them down, but they weren't aware of. Why don't you draw up your own Success Inventory Checklist for the key tasks in your business?

Be consistent

People hate inconsistency. If you're consistent in your handling of situations and don't play favourites, people will naturally respect you.

But human nature being as it is this is easier said than done. It's natural to gravitate towards some people in your company. Some people bring in the lion's share of the revenue and it's easy to favour them or give them more attention. But this creates a very dangerous situation. You must maintain consistency to build a great company.

And in the short term this can cost you money. Top achievers have a natural tendency to want or even expect small favours and more attention — but this can be a trap that many fall into. Just like a parent in a family, it's critical to ensure that all of your team feel there is consistency at the top.

Make sure they tell you what they really think

Every quarter (which I'm still not sure is frequent enough) we send out a list of questions to every team member to gauge team morale.

From people who just started with us yesterday to our longest-standing employee, everyone is asked the same questions.

We send them electronically via our intranet. All responses are anonymous (team members only disclose their regional office and division) so we really get people's true feelings, as painful as that can be!

In Marcus Buckingham and Curt Coffman's book, *FIRST, break all the rules — What the World's Greatest Managers Do Differently*, there is an excellent staff survey which encompasses the following areas: level of day-to-day job satisfaction; workplace commitment to quality, frequency of recognition by management of job well done; regular performance appraisals; pleasant and supportive working environment; and opportunities for professional development. There are many of these sorts of surveys available, but you might like to create your own with your staff that reflects your company's priorities and allows you to highlight areas of growth, support and development.

I encourage my staff to be really aware and open with their attitude toward their working environment, colleagues and the company in general — and these are the sorts of values and issues I ask my employees to reflect on.

- Do they understand their work?

- Are they given regular encouragement?

- Have they got the right tools required to do their job?

- Are their ideas and opinions listened to?

- Do they have good relationships with their colleagues?

- Do they feel they are part of a team?
- Is their progress being monitored?
- Do they enjoy their workplace?
- Are they getting opportunities to learn and develop?

The questions usually take less than 60 seconds to complete on-line. We also encourage everyone to provide any further thoughts on how they think we're running the company and what they'd do differently if they were in charge.

As each team member responds our software collates the results and management can get a good snapshot of staff morale by division or regional office. We display the results graphically, and track and compare the results to previous surveys. This is one of our most important scoreboards and we treat the results just as importantly as we do our profit results and customer feedback.

Give praise at random

We have monthly awards for team members who are performing well. But one of the most effective ways to give praise and reward good performance is to do it randomly and spontaneously.

I'll often stop off at the chocolate shop on the way back from an appointment and buy a few boxes of chocolates. Then I just walk around the office giving them out and chatting for a few minutes. Little things like this make a big difference. They create a sense of fun.

You can also send a few emails around acknowledging people's contribution. Pull up a chair next to someone and have a quick chat, asking how things are going and is there anything you can do for them.

It's very hard to give too much praise — almost impossible. But it's very easy to give too little. So make the effort to constantly applaud small victories. By giving praise and acknowledgment you're creating an environment for achieving bigger victories.

How to deliver criticism effectively

Unfortunately it can't be all praise. Sometimes things don't go as well as they could and you need to give team members some constructive feedback about their performance. You have to be careful, because people can easily take things personally and get upset. You must make it clear that the criticism is aimed not at the person, but at their actions.

I've found the best way to deliver criticism is with a 'praise sandwich'. There are four elements to it:

1. Start with a positive statement about something they've done, or are doing, well.
2. Ask some questions around the issue at hand. Give them the opportunity to bring up the issue themselves — often they'll be a great self-critic.
3. Offer your support or a suggestion on how they can improve.
4. Finish up with some positive feedback.

I'll give you an example. I wanted to talk to one of our operations managers because the presentation at a couple of our offices needed a little attention. So I took her aside where no-one else could listen.

Starting with some positive feedback, I said, 'Lucy, I just wanted to let you know that I went over to Leichhardt the other day and the office is looking fantastic. I think the way you brought that together on time and on budget was great. You've done an excellent job and everyone is really excited. So I wanted to thank you for that.'

Next, I went into questions-mode to give Lucy the opportunity to bring up the issue at hand herself. I asked, 'How do you feel the Eastern suburbs and Lower North Shore offices are presenting?'

She replied, 'I think they really need an upgrade.' So I asked what this would entail. She said, 'I think we need a spring clean and there's a few things we need to get fixed.' And then I gave my input, adding, 'I also noticed there were some shopping trolleys in the carpark the other day — we need to get rid of those.'

It's important to ask questions around the issue rather than make statements about where you think your employee went wrong. By using questions you're engaging in a conversation and they're less likely to flashback to being berated by their parents when they were eight years old.

Next I offered my support by asking if there was anything she needed from me to make the upgrade happen. She said no, she would handle it. Your offer of support is a key part of the praise sandwich. Usually people say they're OK, but by providing an offer of support, it gives them a good feeling because they know they're not alone — help is there if they need it.

Finally I finished up with some more positive feedback. I said, 'So this is a great opportunity to get all the offices looking as beautiful as you've got the Inner West office looking. Keep up the good work and let me know if there's anything I can do.'

One final point: when you need to give someone constructive criticism, do it straight away. The closer your feedback is to the event the better. Because when you say 'Hey, Stephanie, can we talk about what happened last week,' Stephanie's thinking, 'Oh my God, what did I do last week. I can't even remember. Don't tell me he's been waiting a week to tell me I've done something wrong. No wonder he was a bit offhand the other day.' So all of a sudden this craziness in Stephanie's inner dialogue can start happening.

Praise in public, criticise in private

When you want to give feedback to a team member, always praise in public, criticise in private. When you praise staff in front of their peers it makes them feel great and gives a boost to the whole team. And when you need to give constructive criticism to someone, you don't want to embarrass them, so do it out of earshot of the rest of the team.

How to deal with non-team players

With all your accountability and KPIs in place it's not difficult to spot people who are under-performing and take corrective action. A far less obvious but more dangerous threat is team members who undermine your culture: the non-team players. You have to act on them real fast.

I've generally found that if you've got a strong culture and you're direct with people, non-team players won't be comfortable in your environment. So they'll leave of their own accord or change their habits to fit in with the culture.

Deep down people don't want to come to work and be negative. It's a habit they've picked up along the way. They've run out of inspiration and lost the dream. So you have to give them the opportunity to get that spark back.

We'll say, 'Hey, we've noticed that this behaviour is not really in line with what this company's about. So we really want to talk to you about that and get your view of it and work out a way to move forward.' Again, it's not about them, it's about how they're operating: their actions and habits.

Occasionally, I find people aren't even aware they're doing it. They might be constantly complaining, but when confronted say: 'My God, I've never realised I was doing that.' So you have to give them the opportunity to change their ways.

If they're not prepared to change, people will often resign soon after one of these chats. They see the writing on the wall. We've had a few people who've done that and then re-applied three months later. They've thought, 'Oh well, I don't need this place,' and gone elsewhere. But they've found out they miss the culture and the energy.

Some we re-employ and some we don't. We don't have a policy that once you leave, we'll never look at you again. We take a fresh look at them and see if their attitude's really changed.

You can never go wrong telling the truth

Trust that you can never go wrong telling the truth, if you tell it with a positive intention. Don't tell it to embarrass people, don't tell it to make people feel bad, and don't manipulate it to support your position. Tell it to help realise your vision of the business, to get your team involved and to help them to grow and be exceptional in everything they do.

PART FOUR

You+sales

12.

The foundations of sales success

It's a common misconception that some of us are 'born salespeople' and the rest just can't do it. While some people might take to the task more readily than others, your sales ability is not an immutable part of your makeup like green eyes or brown hair. Selling is a learned skill and can be picked up by anybody who is determined enough. And one of the best ways to learn is by studying those who do it well.

The traits of a good salesperson

These days high-performing salespeople come in all shapes and sizes, from a variety of backgrounds, and age and gender are not barriers. There's no such thing as the stereotypical salesperson anymore. However, there are several common traits that I notice in high-performance salespeople, which can be learned and developed over time.

Energy and passion

I think sales is really all about transferring your beliefs, passion and energy for your product or service to your customer. If you passionately believe in your product or service, all you have to do is transfer that belief across to your customer. You don't have to make anything up, you don't have to pretend to be anything, you don't have to over-exaggerate — you just need to pass on your energy and passion for the product.

So part of being a good salesperson is being able to maintain that energy and passion over a sustained period. To be able to consistently deliver day-in day-out, 12 hours a day, you need to be passionate about what you're selling and be able to maintain a high energy level.

Once I was looking for an apartment for myself and I inspected an apartment by Mirvac. I was really impressed by the enthusiasm of the salesman. He genuinely loved the apartment. I could tell that he would love to live there himself. On the way down in the lift I asked how he was enjoying his job. He said, 'I'm just loving it. I'm so proud to work for Mirvac, because they're the best developer in the country.' I was really moved. A lot of employees complain about their work situation, but this young guy was exuding pride and positive energy.

Self-management

When I started in business I was fascinated by McDonald's. It wasn't the food that interested me, but their management and customer service systems. When you walk in the approach is always the same. The standard of cleanliness is generally the same. The time it takes from ordering your food to receiving it is the same.

With this level of service replicated in many businesses, people now expect fast food service even if they're not in McDonald's.

They have a heightened expectation of the speed at which service should be delivered. Speed and efficiency are now the norm, and even if you're not in the fast food industry, your customers expect snappy service from you anyway.

How does this affect salespeople? Most big-ticket item sales environments are not highly supervised, so self-management, creating systems and time management are critical qualities for salespeople to develop.

From my experience this is an area where most salespeople could significantly improve their game. Salespeople are often naturally gifted with high energy, passion and good people skills — that's why they chose a sales career. But the ability to systemise and prioritise is often something they have to learn from scratch.

Consultative approach

In the old days salespeople would hit the customer right between the eyes with a sales pitch listing four or five compelling reasons why they should buy the product. But today's consumer is unlikely to fall for that. People are now very well informed, and with the Internet, becoming even more so.

Rather than have some pre-prepared pitch foisted on them, customers want salespeople to listen to them, customise a solution to their problem, recommend a go-forward plan and then be able to implement it. Rather than telling the customer about what you have to sell, it's about finding out what they really need.

You've got to take a consultative approach with people. Drill into where the customer is in their buying cycle. What are their issues and concerns? What experience have they had in the past dealing in this area? What are they worried about in going forward? What issues do they have about your company or you? What are the outcomes they'd like to achieve? What's their timeframe?

Engage your customer in the process rather than try and shove some pre-determined package in their direction. Use a questions-based presentation rather than a statements-based presentation and listen carefully to what your customer has to say.

Determination

Most sales aren't made on the first or second call. They're more often made on the fifth, tenth or fifteenth call. There can be a lot of no's before you get a yes.

In the face of repeated rejections, a lot of salespeople give up too soon. They call a couple of times, get a couple of rejections and stop calling. They rationalise to themselves, 'If Mrs Baker wants to deal with me, I'll guess she'll give me a call.' But Mrs Baker is busy, she's got other things on her mind, she's considering other proposals, she's got a wedding on this Saturday — all sorts of things are happening.

To excel at sales you've got to develop old-fashioned determination to stick with it in the face of repeated knock-backs from customers who might not be ready to buy your product yet.

Dealing with rejection

One of the major factors for building determination is your ability to handle rejection. You've just got to accept it's part of the process and not take it personally.

It's helpful to reframe what that rejection means to you. In my world, rejection is simply a precursor to success. I know that in my quest to achieve a particular goal I'm probably going to have to get rejected and fail along the way. I just know it's part of the process, so I'm geared up for it, mentally and emotionally. So rather than seeing rejection as something dire and to be avoided, I embrace it as an inevitable part of achieving my goals. Each rejection just brings me closer to success.

Just because you experience some rejection and failure doesn't guarantee you will be successful at achieving a goal. But I've got to tell you, you'll never be successful without having some rejections, failures and setbacks along the way.

Once you see failure, challenges, non-desired outcomes and hurdles as just a normal part of the process, you can prepare yourself for them. I once read a great book called *The Positive Power of Negative Thinking* which explains how to do this. If you sit down and list all the things that can possibly go wrong then there are no surprises if they do go wrong. Furthermore, you can then take steps to deal with every eventuality.

So if you're prospecting and you make an hour's worth of calls, don't expect five out of 10 of them to embrace you and say yes. Know that you've only got to find one person that's actually in a position and willing to do business today to make it a successful prospecting session.

A desire to do better

All good salespeople that I come across have some sort of in-built competitiveness with themselves. They're not necessarily competitive with their colleagues or competitors, but more concerned with how can I do better this month, how can I provide a better service, *how can I do an extra three or four deals this month, how can I find another 10 customers this month?*

They've got an internal radar that's always searching for a higher level of performance. I think we all have this feeling of driving yourself and wanting to do better and wanting to provide more, but some people have a higher awareness of it and utilise it better.

Customer focus

Every time I meet a customer I want them to leave the meeting saying that was the best service experience of their life. That's my philosophy. If I focus on that every single day, with every phone call I make and every customer I meet, it will have a huge impact on my results.

This is the mindset a good salesperson should cultivate — really wanting to over-deliver to your customers. Your inner dialogue should constantly be considering how to turn this customer into a raving fan.

Personal presentation

Personal presentation isn't such a big issue for salespeople these days because customers are used to different styles from formal to casual. The most important aspect of presentation – aside from the obvious need to maintain a high standard of personal hygiene and cleanliness – is dressing appropriately for your market. There's no one presentation that will be right for all situations. If you're selling livestock in the bush, your presentation is going to be different to selling real estate in the CBD.

An ability to work hard

In the early days of my career I was working 80 hours a week. I don't necessarily recommend that work program to other people, but I do believe that in the early phase of a sales career or business you need to put in the hard yards. You've got to come in an hour early and make some extra phone calls, and you've often got to stay after hours to follow up.

However, once you've built some momentum you will get to a point where you can achieve far more with far less. But that's not usually on day one or day 30. It's usually at least a year down the track. So until you've built that momentum you've got to be prepared to work hard.

Positive self belief

Salespeople who achieve a lot have an absolute belief they can achieve a lot. They've generally got strong self-esteem and confidence.

It's a really fine line between confidence and arrogance. If you step over the line your sales career will start plummeting, because people hate arrogant salespeople. But you have to be confident in your ability and what you can deliver to people.

Self-assessment

James Dack is our company's longest-standing team member. He is recognised as one of the most successful real estate agents in Australia. His advice for anyone considering a career in sales is to do a thorough self-evaluation to see if you have the right skills and attitudes:

'It's really important to have a good look at yourself – and you've got to be brutally honest. Do a self-assessment and see how you come up.

'The hardest thing for anybody is to look in the mirror and be critical of themselves. Everyone spends time in front of the mirror combing their hair and making themselves look good on the outside. But you have to look on the inside, and ask yourself:

'Am I the sort of person that is diligent about being on time? Do I tell the truth all the time? Am I the sort of person who likes talking and not listening? Do I really hear what the other person has to say? Do I have good organisational skills? Can I put myself in someone else's shoes and understand where they're coming from?

'It's also helpful to get some feedback about yourself from the people closest to you. Ask someone you can trust such as a sibling or your best friend. You might ask your partner, "Do I listen to you enough?" You might be surprised when they say, "I'm glad you asked that question, because no, you don't. Mostly you just talk and don't listen."

'The most crucial thing is to identify the areas you need to work on. Once you have this awareness it's not too difficult to find someone to help you improve.'

Filling the pipeline

If your business is flat today, it probably means you weren't prospecting enough 90 days ago. Prospecting creates the pipeline for future business — it lays the foundations for tomorrow's sales successes.

Prospecting comes in a variety of forms. The best way to create future business is word of mouth — treating every new customer like gold, and giving incredible service to your current customers. They'll go out and tell others about the great service you've given them and some of those people will then want to do business with you. This is your best conduit to future customers. I'll discuss word of mouth marketing a bit later in the book.

The best prospects are what I call pipeline customers: people that you know are ready to do business. They've put their hands up and said they're going to do business soon, it's just a matter of who with, and when. These prospects are sourced from referrals or leads you've come across. Keep a database of pipeline customers and put them at the top of your list when you make prospecting calls.

Another source of prospects is past clients. When I was selling I knew that if I rang three to five past clients a day, I would contact all of my past clients once or twice a year. I'd say something like: 'Hey, I just drove past your home, the garden looks great, how are things? Pop by the office some time and say hi.' Making this small effort goes a long way to maintaining a good ongoing relationship, and improving the chances of doing business again.

The next group of prospects is your centres of influence. These are people who have the ability to refer multiple customers to you. For me it was accountants, solicitors, architects and financial advisers — people who were dealing with a large

Darren Shirlaw's distribution model

There's nothing wrong with building your client base one person at a time using word of mouth – that's a solid marketing plan. But if you really want to move your business along you should consider developing a distribution model. Let me give you an example:

Kelloggs manufacture a great line of breakfast cereals, but imagine if they tried to find and sell to each consumer one-by-one, household to household. It would be too time consuming. They would be unlikely to prosper. So instead they go to supermarket chains, because that's where lots of people who want to buy cereal will be. Kelloggs can leverage that traffic and create a distribution channel.

So what are your potential distribution channels? To find this out think about how customers find you. Where do they typically first make contact with your firm? What other stuff is happening at the same time that they're involved with your product?

In real estate, we came up with about 30 things that people need or are involved with when they're buying a new home. They visit a solicitor to get a contract prepared. They get their finances organised with a bank manager, mortgage broker or accountant. If they're moving because they've got a job transfer they may be working with recruitment or relocation companies, and so on.

By developing relationships with these centres of influence we created a vast network of potential referrals. It's a mutually beneficial arrangement, because we also refer our customers back to these centres of influence.

number of potential customers in my business. I'd create relationships with them and meet on a regular basis. I'd take them to breakfast, send them updates on what's happening in the market and send them clients.

I would also prospect my competitors' dissatisfied customers. I'd often hear on the grapevine about people that were unable to sell through other agents. I might have actually lost their business initially, and they had gone to another agent and been unsuccessful. I'd make a list of these people and be really focused on following up with them. A missed opportunity might only be temporary. There's often great potential for you to come back and get their business second time around.

This leads to my 'second in line strategy'. Often I knew of someone that had a long-standing relationship with an agent in my area, who had no real reason to start doing business with me at this time. But if they did decide to change agents, I wanted them to change to me. So I'd build a relationship with them anyway, so in the event they had a falling out with their current agents, I'd be the first person they thought of.

Effective prospecting tips

The best advice I can give you about prospecting is (like the Nike slogan) 'just do it'. Stop putting it off, put this book down right now, and make some prospecting calls!

OK, so that's pretty obvious. But even though most businesspeople recognise the importance of prospecting, they avoid doing it. They make excuses to themselves, procrastinate and cross their fingers hoping new clients will miraculously appear.

Suddenly money is short, customers are scarce and you can procrastinate no longer. But when you're short of business it's the worst time to prospect. People can hear the desperation. The best time to prospect is when you have a lot of business, because you've got the momentum and confidence.

Prospecting essentials

For successful prospecting follow these four steps:

1. Recognise that tomorrow's sales come from today's prospecting.

2. Diarise your prospecting appointments.

3. Have your prospecting list handy.

4. Know what you're going to say and have fun saying it!

Recognise the importance of prospecting

Good prospectors know that the phone is their friend. Depending on your business, I'd recommend devoting one to two hours to phoning prospects every day.

To help get you motivated you must start with the right mental framework. Remind yourself that prospecting is about generating leads that create business down the track. It's an investment in your business that will pay dividends in the future. Prospecting is an essential activity for anyone who wants to build their business.

Make prospecting appointments

Prospecting is as important as your sales appointments. You can't do one without the other. I'm sure that you'd be unlikely to miss a sales appointment. You wouldn't procrastinate about preparing a sales presentation. Yet many people put off prospecting indefinitely.

The trick is to make appointments for prospecting, because we don't usually miss appointments. Prospecting is not something that you just fit in where you can (i.e. 'I'll get around to it some time'). It's important enough to deserve an appointment. So block out some time in your diary for prospecting.

When I was selling there were two things in my diary I had to do every morning. Firstly I'd ring all of my current clients to touch base with them, just to check that they're okay and give them an update. And then I'd do one to two hours prospecting each day on top of that.

Unless you put prospecting into your schedule, you're always going to find reasons not to do it.

Make it fun

Prospecting is a bit like exercising. It's hard to overcome the inertia at first and often there's a little pain. But once you get into a regular habit it actually ain't that bad!

And like exercise, prospecting is easier if you make it fun. My attitude was that it's just meeting new people on the phone. Even if they weren't interested in my services, it was still a great opportunity for me to meet people.

One of the greatest prospectors I ever saw was working for a real estate company in Toronto. He made a little ritual of his daily prospecting, starting by getting himself physically and mentally ready. He would get himself set up with his phone headset because he liked to make his calls standing up.

On the walls of his office he had pictures of his wife and family, and holiday destinations he wanted to visit. These inspired him and helped him to focus on the goals he wanted to achieve. He knew that every call was helping to provide for his family and moving him closer to his goals.

I know some people who give themselves rewards for a completed prospecting session. They might love cappuccinos, so they say *after 50 calls I'm going to get a cappuccino from the café — that's my reward.*

Another strategy is to buddy up and prospect with someone else. You could say to one of your colleagues, 'Hey, why don't we meet every morning at 8.30 a.m. and do 30 minutes of prospecting calls, and we'll have a race to see who can get the best leads. Then we'll go to the café and have a cup of coffee.' So you can make it a fun activity that you can share with someone else.

So instead of procrastinating, channel the energy you've been putting into creative avoidance into creating a fun prospecting ritual. Once you get a prospecting habit and it becomes part of your daily routine, you'll actually start to look forward to it.

Every no moves you closer to a yes

Unless you accept that the majority of people you prospect are not going to be ready to do business with you, you're going to find it emotionally too tough to go through that rejection barrier.

I had an expectation that for most people I'd call, the timing wouldn't be right for them to do business with me at that moment. So I'd prepare myself mentally up front. Then I wouldn't get upset when people said 'No, I don't want to buy a house from you' or 'No, I don't want to sell a house through you at the moment.'

I used to connect the rejection associated with prospecting with the success I'd ultimately achieve. I realised that I'd have to ring 50 people to get one to say yes. And if I wanted four to say yes, I'd have to make 200 calls.

You need to remind yourself that the no's you get along the way are part of the road to yes and your ultimate success.

Your prospecting list

Before you get on the phone you must create an easy access trail to your prospecting list. (I've already discussed who to put on your prospecting list in 'Filling the pipeline', above.) Get a printout with all the contact names and numbers of the people who you intend to call each day.

For your own sake prioritise your prospect lists. It's obviously preferable to make 50 calls and get a yes, rather than make 500 calls to get a yes. So always refine your lists and start with prospects you have some connection and relevance to.

Your prospecting script

Another reason why people resist prospecting is because they don't know what to say. Your guiding principle is always: what's in it for them? Rather than telling your prospects how good you are, tell them about some relevant benefits you can offer them.

One of my sales calls might have sounded like this: 'Anne, I just wanted to give you a little bit of an update on some of the sales that are happening in your street at the moment, because there have been some really good results.

'I just thought you might be a little bit excited to hear that the house three doors away just sold for $1 million, and I know you bought yours for $480,000 about three years ago, so I thought I'd give you a call.

'The other thing is, a couple of people that I looked after at the same time you bought your place are moving houses at the moment, and I wondered whether you're interested in me looking for another property for you at all? Do you need any more space or are you looking for a change?'

So my focus was always on *how can I help you?* In summary, I kept my scripts simple, direct, questions-based and focused on the customer.

You also need to have a reasonably clear outcome for the call. A lot of my prospecting calls would take less than 30 seconds. I'd pretty quickly realise whether I could be any help to them or whether they were looking for any assistance or support, and the phone call would go in one of two directions.

If they were interested in my services it would be an extended call. Otherwise it would be, 'Thanks very much for that. Do you mind if I pop a card in the post just so you've got my details if you ever do need anything?'

It's nice to be best, but it's imperative to be there

Stephen Bradbury became famous when he won Australia's first gold medal at a Winter Olympics for the men's 1000-metre speed ice-skating in 2002. Bradbury was far from the strongest skater in the final and only had an outside chance of winning a medal. But when the first four skaters crashed into each other, he skated past them to win gold.

After the event the press asked him what his strategy was. He said, 'To be there, to skate as fast as I could and hope everybody else fell over!' And that's exactly what happened. Bradbury wasn't the fastest skater on the rink, but he did show up. The same principle applies to salespeople.

When I'm presenting sales talks I often ask the audience, 'Hands up anyone that has bought a product from someone that they didn't like?' Invariably most of the people in the auditorium put their hands up. Why do we buy things from people we don't like? Because we needed the product and they were the only ones there at the time.

So while it's important to develop the best product you can, and aim for outstanding customer service, it's even more important to be there. You have to be there when the customer is making a decision, you have to be out there talking to people, generating business and developing distribution channels. Because you don't always have to be the best, but you do have to be there.

Some people will be reading this book thinking something like this: 'I don't work for IBM. I work for Compaq, and to be honest, I don't think Compaq has as good a product as IBM.' It really doesn't matter, because people buy IBM and people buy Compaq. If you're there demonstrating the features and benefits of your computer, giving the best customer service you can and answering the customer's queries, chances are they'll buy your computer even if it isn't the best, because the guy who's selling the best computer never returned their phone call.

The moral of this story is don't feel that you're at a disadvantage just because you don't think you're the best salesperson in the country, or that your product or company is not the best. If you're there, you've already got an enormous advantage.

I read a survey a long time ago that said one in three professional services people that are called for a quotation or to discuss business, never return the call. So you're in great shape just by being there and answering the phone!

What worked today?

A lot of salespeople follow what I call the 'fly strategy'. You know when you see a fly and it wants to get outside but it flies straight into a window. So what does it do? The fly goes back and flies even harder into the window. And when it still can't get through, it goes back and flies in really hard, and just ends up with a headache.

In sales, as in life, the fly strategy just doesn't work. If something's not working you don't just keep going harder at it. You need to find a smarter way to achieve your goal. So at the end of each day or the end of each appointment, ask yourself these two questions:

What worked today?
What's not right yet?

I used to do a quick review after every sales appointment. I'd sit in my car for five minutes and think about the objections the customers raised that I didn't have an appropriate response for. What statistics did they want that I didn't have? What things do I have to get back to them about that I could have told them on the spot? If I could rewind the videotape by an hour, what would I have done differently?

Often I'd also ask them outright what I could have done better, especially if I didn't get the business. I'd say to them, 'Hamish, just let me know what it is that you don't feel comfortable with, or what could I have done better, because I really wanted your business'.

I found people would give me phenomenal feedback. Sometimes they were so impressed by my honesty, and that I cared so much about meeting their needs, that they'd reconsider and give me their business. In any case, their feedback would help me to get the next piece of business I went for.

Business as usual is no longer an option

According to futurists, the world will change more in the next 20 years than it did in the last 100. This rapid change presents opportunities for small business to capture large markets.

'Upstarts and entrepreneurs love change. Turbulence scrambles up the pieces on the game board and gives them a chance to gain market share and profits.' SETH GODIN

13.

Making the sale

While I believe some people are more naturally gifted in the world of sales, I also strongly believe that becoming an excellent salesperson is merely a matter of developing several key skills and applying them consistently.

I was certainly not a natural born salesperson. I was shy, awkward and not at all predisposed to becoming a salesperson. I had to work hard to develop any fluency at all, but it was worth the effort that it took to acquire the skills necessary to sell anything.

In this chapter I have outlined some key skills and techniques you must master to become the best in the world of selling in any industry. But first, here's what not to do:

Six major sales mistakes

Put these dirty half dozen on your To Don't list and you'll be well on your way to a stellar sales career.

1. Not following through on promises

Always follow through on promises. You build your reputation, relationships, business and brand on integrity and following through on every promise you make. It's critical.

Don't make a commitment unless you're able to deliver on it. Too many salespeople say, 'Yeah, I'll have that over to you in 30 minutes,' or 'Yeah, we can deliver that on the 1st, that'll be no problem,' when they don't know whether it's possible.

2. Communication – not keeping in touch

The number one complaint I hear from customers about salespeople in any industry is that they don't keep them informed. So find a routine to keep in touch with your customers. Always be a caller, not a callee. Over-communicate with your customers. Tell them what you are going to do, tell them when you're doing it, and then tell them when you've done it.

3. Not handling and resolving conflict

Conflicts never get smaller — they always get bigger, until they're taken care of. So tackle conflicts straight away. Seize the opportunity to build a stronger relationship with your customer. Go hard on the truth, tell them the way it is, and then tell them how you will resolve the issue.

4. Not setting and managing expectations

It's very rare for salespeople to sit their customers down and outline any potential pitfalls with the sale. But it's a vital process to ensure they have realistic expectations.

When I was selling real estate, I'd say to clients, 'The average time on the market for the properties I handle is 30 days. I also need to let you know that some clients' homes are on the market for six months. But sometimes the first person we bring through buys the home.' So I managed the client's expectations around the uncertain timeframe for selling their home. But many agents wouldn't do this. So when the house hasn't sold after seven weeks the client gets disappointed and angry with the agent.

5. Crisis management versus time management

Most salespeople focus their attention and energy on the most immediate, urgent, challenging squeaking door, but that's rarely the best place to have your focus day to day. Obviously crises will come up and do need to be managed in a timely fashion.

However, too many salespeople become adrenalin junkies and they specialise in crisis management. You must create a system to handle crises efficiently, but your main focus should be on activities that move the business forward.

6. Blaming and excuses

People want to blame every single thing except themselves for undesired outcomes. Major mistake. What you need to do is accept responsibility, even for things that appear to be beyond your control.

Your event got washed out and you lost money, how are you responsible for that? You can't control the weather, but you didn't have a bad weather plan for the event, so that was your problem. You should have put a deposit down on an alternative venue. You might have made slightly less profit, but consider it your insurance policy.

The bubble theory

Larry Emdur is a friend of mine and he's developed a great strategy he calls 'the bubble theory'. When you're with a customer you create an imaginary bubble that covers just you and the customer. You shield yourself from any external issues you have and focus your attention solely on the customer and your task at hand.

You can have all sorts of pressing concerns in the world outside. You've had an argument at home with your partner. You've got something you have to do later that you're dreading. Whatever. But during those 30 seconds or 25 minutes it's just you and the customer in the bubble. No other distractions, no other negative energy around.

This is a great technique to use with all your interactions, including with your manager, boss, employees, and even your friends and family outside work.

The last three feet

Another great technique I picked up from Larry Emdur is 'the last three feet'. It's about giving a great first impression and making the most of that tiny window of opportunity.

Larry developed this technique when he was doing some training for pharmaceutical salespeople. He asked them to talk him through a typical sales call. They told him, 'When we have a new drug coming out we ring up the surgery and make an appointment to meet the doctor. She's really busy and doesn't really want to be schmoozed by a sales rep, but we manage to make an appointment anyway. Then we're waiting in the foyer with all the patients. When they're all done the doctor opens the door and says, "Hello — please come in".'

This is the crucial moment. Because in those last three feet, from standing up, stepping forward and shaking the doctor's hand, they have to make a connection. Their appearance, their energy, their smile, their handshake and the first five words they say are crucial. They can have done all the preparation in the world, have a fantastic presentation and flawless product knowledge, but if they blow the last three feet, they can blow the sale in an instant.

You've got to recognise these key moments in the sales process — the last three feet — and be prepared for them. Don't look messy and disorganised. Don't be tired. Don't smell of alcohol or garlic. Don't blow it! You've got to make immediate impact, create immediate rapport, be concise and get straight to the issue.

Gathering momentum

The greatest enemy of any salesperson is inertia. Getting rolling in the direction of your goals from a standing start is where much of the challenge lies. Once you've achieved some momentum it's much easier to move from low volume sales to high volume, but many people never get past the starting line.

Making world-class presentations

Over the years I've delivered lots of sales presentations and I've learned some useful tips and techniques. I'd like to share some of them with you.

Be prepared

Without adequate preparation it's almost impossible to deliver a world-class presentation. I don't mean learning a presentation by rote. What you need to prepare for is overcoming the major obstacle between you and a sale: any of your customer's concerns, issues and reservations.

You probably have a good idea what these are already. Draw up a list of questions that are likely to unearth any issues the customer may have. You can run through some of these questions with the customer when you're making an appointment.

I had 12 questions that I'd ask, such as: What's your timing? Have you sold a property before? What was that experience like? Do you have any specific things that you would like me to prepare or discuss at the meeting? How much time are you going to have when we meet?

Once I knew what the issues were I could prepare myself to address them. Typically I'd prepare for at least one hour prior to the presentation. I'd gather any information, case studies and statistics that would be useful for addressing the issues of that particular client.

I would also take a moment to mentally rehearse the presentation. I'd visualise what an outstanding outcome was going to look like. I'd visualise getting on really well with the customer and building good rapport. I'd visualise being comfortable handling any of the issues that might arise. I'd visualise myself clearly articulating our service proposition. Ultimately, I'd visualise walking out of the house with a signed agreement, then a *for sale* sign, and finally a *sold* sign.

The power of visualisation

Many years ago someone sent me a postcard of a beautiful hotel lobby. I kept it and pasted it into my success journal because it looked like the sort of place I'd love to stay when I had a bit more money. Years later I was in the US for a real estate workshop and I checked into the Four Seasons Hotel in Chicago. I'd never been there before, but it seemed very familiar. I had an eerie feeling of déjà vu.

Some time after that, I was looking through my success journal and saw the postcard of the beautiful hotel lobby. Guess what? It was the Four Seasons in Chicago. It just goes to show the power of visualisation.

In my mind I was already hired. And it was amazing how many times everything turned out as I'd visualised.

Make your presentations customer-centric

The most important requirement of your presentation is that it must be customer-centric. Put yourself into your customers' shoes. They need to be clear about, 'What's in it for me?' If your presentation addresses that question you're well on your way to making a sale.

I often see brochures from real estate agents with their name plastered all over them, what they have achieved and how professional they are. But when I read them from the point of view of a potential customer, I can't see any clearly defined benefit for me. Refocus on the customer, not on you.

When you're delivering a sales presentation or creating a marketing brochure, you have to spell out clearly what benefits your customers will receive by dealing with you. Every single piece of sales collateral and your entire sales presentation should be centred on articulating the benefits and advantages you're offering the customer.

Practice makes perfect

Once you've got your list of likely customer concerns, issues and reservations you need to get comfortable with handling them as they arise in the real world. I suggest you do this initially by role-playing with someone other than your customers.

When I started my real estate business 15 years ago I used to do role-plays in front of a video camera with a colleague. At the end of the day when we'd finished with all the customers and made all our calls, we would sit down and role-play for half an hour. He would give me some objections I'd most likely receive the next day, or ones I'd actually received that day, and I'd practise my responses to them. Then we'd swap roles.

By practising I became more comfortable with customers raising objections or issues. I could give a totally natural response — it didn't sound canned, it didn't feel canned. I knew that people would have these issues and I knew that I'd dealt with them in my role-plays, so it was much easier to deal with them as they arose with customers.

It's not about faking it — it's about simulating a sales scenario so you can perfect your performance. It's like a sporting team having a practice match on Thursday night against the reserve team. They're getting ready for when they face the real opponents.

The aim is to get comfortable with dealing with customers' issues without any undue anxiety. You want your responses to be second nature, without sounding or feeling forced or unnatural.

The more you practise them, the more you internalise them, and the more natural they will sound and feel. Perhaps the first few times you use some of the responses you've been practising you might feel a bit unnatural. That might make your customer uncomfortable and it might cost you a sale. But it's just like learning to ride a bike — you've got to fall off a few times before you get good at it.

You're never too good to practise

If you're a sales professional with a well-established career you might think you've got your presentations down pat and don't need practice. Well, from my experience the best people keep practising. They never get to a point where they think they've got it all in the bag.

Bob Bohlen, from Brighton, Michigan, is the number one real estate salesperson in the world. His team (who are some of the best salespeople around) practise their sales scripts for 45 minutes every single morning, between 8.30 a.m. and 9.15 am.

Statistics

Always have a few relevant statistics that relate to the customer. Customers are impressed by statistics, because they demonstrate you have done your research and know what you're talking about. Also, the information is often enlightening to them.

When I was selling property I'd know the percentage of buyers in a suburb who came from that area. I'd say, 'One of the things that's really important to know before we develop a marketing plan is that around 82% of potential buyers will come from within seven kilometres of where we're sitting tonight.' That would help my customers understand the process and at the same time build confidence that I was competent and professional, and really knew what I was talking about. It can set you apart.

Case studies

Case studies are also very useful. They act as a form of social proof and can help customers to overcome any reservations they may have. I'd always have a real life case study for each of the four or five most likely customer issues.

For example, someone might say, 'I'm not really sure if we should auction on-site, every other agent I've spoken to says auction in a boardroom'. So I'd say, 'I really understand that. I know that a lot of other agents recommend boardroom auctions, but let me tell you about a recent experience we had with an on-site auction and how well it worked. We got a fantastic result that we wouldn't have got in the boardroom...'

So whatever the likely issues are going to be, it's good to have relevant case studies to reassure your customers.

Visuals

I always use visuals in my presentations. It's true, a picture's worth a thousand words. You should utilise images to help communicate your message more efficiently.

I had a little Kodak pouch with photographs and images that would illustrate some of the points I was talking about. For example, if a customer was unsure about having an on-site auction, I'd show them a photo I had of an on-site auction I did at Clovelly. It was a little semi. There must have been 150 people there. You couldn't see a blade of grass on the lawn, they were sitting on the fence, people everywhere! We got a record price for it.

So I'd pull the photo out, hand it to them, and say, 'I'm really glad you raised the issue of where we'll do the auction.' And then I'd explain why I thought an on-site auction was best. This really helped to make them feel more comfortable.

Your visuals don't necessarily have to be super slick either. My Clovelly photo was a snap a friend of mine took, with the date written on the back. More like a holiday snapshot than something from a professional photo shoot. It was real and my customers could see that. It wasn't in a glossy brochure that people tend to doubt.

You should also create your visuals so that people can actually hold them in their hands. It helps get them involved in the sales process and makes it a bit more fun.

Have a think about what visuals or images you can use to enhance your presentations. You should also include some graphs or charts to illustrate the statistics you want to talk about.

Get organised

Nowadays speed is an increasingly important consideration on customers' minds. A rapid response and follow-up to customer enquiries is a great way to set yourself apart from your competition. Speed comes from organisation. Salespeople have to be highly organised. Everything must be ready in advance of your presentation. You need your sales tools, sales collateral, time management tools and support team. Everybody has to be in sync, everybody has to be aligned, and everything has to be accessible.

Arrive five minutes early

I always like to arrive five minutes early for a presentation. It shows I'm punctual and keen. Three to five minutes early is just right. If you get there ten to fifteen minutes early you can actually catch them by surprise which is not a great start.

Set the agenda

When you're with the customer the first thing to do is set the agenda. This helps them to get comfortable. Outline the items that you intend to cover. Then you should ask them if they have any specific questions or issues they want to discuss. I'd say, 'I'm sure there's a few questions you have or issues you'd like to discuss with me. I'd like to know what they might be so we can make sure we handle those.'

Make a note of their queries and issues so you cover them during your presentation.

Building rapport

It's important to make your customers feel comfortable by building rapport with them. Building rapport is about showing them you're on their wavelength and are sympathetic to their needs.

People feel comfortable dealing with someone who is like them. So a great way to build rapport is to mirror the customer. There are several ways to do this. You can mirror their pace. If they're a fast moving person, I'd move my presentation up a few notches. If they had a little slower pace, I'd slow down a bit.

If you're dealing with an analytical type you might focus more on statistics and the fine details. If they're more artistically minded you could focus on your visuals and a creative marketing plan. You can also mirror their language. Do they speak formally or informally?

People sometimes ask me what my sales style is. I tell them it depends who I'm talking to, because whatever makes them feel comfortable is how I will sell to them. Fast or slow, formal or informal.

Ask questions and make recommendations

I always use a questions-based presentation (in case you hadn't already noticed!). Salespeople often screw up because they have a statements-based presentation. They deliver their standard presentation and hope someone bites. They focus too much on selling themselves instead of finding what the customer needs to know to make the decision to buy from them.

When I made a presentation I'd assume right from the start that I'd be getting the business. You really have to, because if you think otherwise, why are you there? So it's not a question of selling myself to them, but of dealing with any issues and concerns they might have had about doing business with me.

One of the questions I usually ask up front is: 'What are the most important things for you in selling your property and appointing an agent?' That could elicit anything from 'I'm not sure...' to a one-hour real estate horror story. 'We were ripped off last time. They promised the world, but delivered nothing. They over charged us. My cousin told me never to trust real estate agents.' Whatever it may be, it's best to find out up front.

It's really important to unearth their core issues by asking the right questions. Use open-ended questions to make sure you allow people to expand on their thoughts.

Once you've asked the right questions and you know what the customer's issues and concerns are, you're in a position to offer professional recommendations that they can say yes or no to.

Confirming not closing

In old-fashioned selling they talk about 'closing the sale'. But for me it's not closing, it's confirming the recommendations I'd made during the presentation as I'd been addressing the customer's issues.

At some stage you have to shift gears — obviously at your customer's pace — and find out what their decision is. You need to ask the questions to confirm the recommendations you've discussed.

I might say something like, 'So, we've talked about auctioning the property, how does that sit with you? You said you can't move for 90 days, so I suggest we start on January 1. Does that work for you? Open inspections — you mentioned the house looks best in the mornings, so let's say 10 to 11 on Thursdays and Saturdays. Is that any good?'

At the end of your presentation there are three possible outcomes: either you've got their business, or they've decided to go with someone else, or there are still some issues to be resolved. You should try to end up with a decision either way rather than be left with indecision.

Often at the beginning of a presentation I'd say, 'At the end of this there are a few decisions that you can make, and you just need to know that I'm really comfortable with whichever way you want to go. If you want to enlist our company and have me work with you, I'd be delighted because this is really the sort of house I like selling. If you decide my company isn't right for you or you don't feel comfortable with me representing you, I'm fine with that decision too. But looking at your timeframe that we talked about on the phone, it's probably best if we make a decision today, either way.'

In this way I'd make them feel really comfortable about saying no, but I'd also be subtly saying, 'Let's make a decision at the end.'

I don't see myself as any more courageous than anyone else on the planet, but I know there are certain 10 to 15 second windows where you have to dig deep. You have to make a recommendation that you know someone might not want to hear. You need to ask a question that you know you might get rejected on.

So I'd steel myself, realise I only had to be courageous for 15 seconds and ask the big question. 'So how do you feel about all that? Would you be comfortable with me selling your home?'

The 10 seconds that count

Jose Canseco is an American baseball star who averaged around 30 home runs a season. For this he was paid millions of dollars. In an interview he said, 'Each home run takes 10 seconds. Everything else is preparation of no commercial value to anybody.' He knew that when he stood up at the plate, he had to be outstanding for the next 10 seconds.

It's the same in sales. A lot of salespeople work 60 hours per week, but there are only about three or four hours that count. That's when you're face to face with the customer closing a deal, negotiating a sale, pitching for business. You're not paid to do paperwork. Make sure you're operating at optimum capacity when you step up to the plate.

How to overcome nerves before a big presentation

Remember to breathe. No, seriously! Just focus on where you are right now and relax.

Also, don't take yourself too seriously. You can be fiercely competitive. Get incredibly excited about every customer you're dealing with. But put things in perspective. Of course you want to make a sale with every presentation, but missing a few isn't going to change your life.

I was intensely competitive and excited about getting every piece of business I could. But I'd also focus on all the benefits I'd gain if this sale didn't come off — like learning to handle rejection — and all the other good stuff that was happening in my life that I could be grateful for.

Following up

Once you've sold someone your product, or they've enlisted your services, invariably they're going to get cold feet soon after. So shortly after you've made the sale it's important to get in touch and reconfirm the benefits of the decision they've just made.

If someone had chosen me to sell their house I'd give them a call the next day to minimise the anxiety they might feel after having made such a big decision. Sometimes they might have spoken to the other agents who lost out. 'The other agent said that you guys were too busy to do a good job and they would have done it for half the price you're asking.'

I'd calmly reply, 'This is exactly the sort of stuff I'd expect them to say. They're upset they didn't get the business. I can really relate to that, but just let me just re-confirm why I think you chose our firm...' And I'd go through it calmly and intelligently and they'd relax again and go to bed happy.

Never tell someone about the features

People don't buy a product or service because of its features. They buy it because of the benefits it gives them. Take a car for example. One of its features might be airbags. But the benefit is keeping the passengers safe. That's why someone will buy the car — because it keeps their family safe.

You need to know the features of your product or service and you need to be able to articulate them clearly, but what you should really be telling your customers about are the benefits.

Our website lists properties we are selling and gets 1.7 million hits a month. But what's important to our customers is that when we list their home for sale on our site we may well get enquiries from New York and London. Those buyers will be bidding in pounds or US dollars, which means the seller can get a better price on auction day.

The feature is the website, but the benefit is more money for your home.

The key influencers

Everything you say and everything you do will influence a customer's decision-making process in some way. However there are four key influencers that I believe have the strongest impact in the selling process.

1. Social proof

When people are uncertain about making a decision they tend to be heavily influenced by the successful decisions others have made in the same circumstances. This is why referrals and word of mouth are the strongest sources of business for any salesperson. People feel most comfortable doing business with someone that one of their friends or colleagues has already done business with.

One of IBM's marketing campaigns in the 1980s used the tagline 'No-one ever got fired for buying an IBM'. This gave potential customers the comfort that IBM was a safe choice that other people had successfully made. Computer sales went through the roof as people followed the tried and tested IBM path rather than taking a perceived risk with other brands.

Testimonials and case studies are also a great way to use social proof to help customers to decide to buy from you.

2. People do business with people they like

We've all done this in the past. We're offered a better deal, but we find a reason to justify why we should buy with the salesperson we like. There's nothing wrong with having 'people I like' as a selection criterion, because if we like them we're more likely to trust them and if we trust them we'll enjoy the process much more.

So when you're selling, an important element in the process is building rapport with the customer and developing a relationship of understanding. This is usually best achieved by asking quality questions and listening actively to the answers.

When I say actively listening I mean really listening to their responses (and not just waiting for your turn to speak!). Understand their concerns. Make sure your recommendation is best for them not just for you. This approach will inevitably win over the customer's trust and dramatically increase your likelihood of winning their business.

3. Scarcity

People generally want something more if they can't have it or if there's only a limited supply. It makes the offering seem so much more special and creates a sense of urgency to act now, before they miss out.

How do you create a sense of urgency in a sales environment? For some people it's a natural situation. If you're operating at the top end of most markets there are usually very limited choices and tightly controlled stock. The current wait for a new model Rolls Royce in most countries is in excess of 12 months!

But for others who deal in more of a commodity market it's more difficult. What I used to do was create self-imposed restrictions on what I did. I knew I could only handle a dozen clients really well at any one time, so I'd set the limit at that. And when someone contacted me to discuss selling their property I'd tell them that I couldn't take on their business right now for the reason just explained, but I'd have an opening within a week or two if they were prepared to wait.

I can tell you I always had a line of customers ready to do business for over fifteen years, partly as a result of the fact that I was selective in how many I'd handle simultaneously.

4. Reciprocity

If you add value to someone, they inevitably want to return the favour. So how does that work in sales? Whenever I got a lead on a customer, I'd try to add so much value to our relationship up front — before they actually needed an agent — that by the time they were ready to sell their house, choosing me was a natural consequence.

When I met someone at an *open for inspection*, I'd give them as much information and advice as I could. I'd help them understand the market, send them relevant magazines or newsletters and refer them to other service providers they might need. I'd provide significant value, so when it was time for them to choose an agent for the sale of their property, they felt very comfortable choosing me. Not that they felt an obligation to pay me back. It's just a natural response to someone adding value.

Overcoming customers' objections, fears and concerns

Customers may be emotionally inclined towards a product or service, but they're often in need of intellectual support to get them over their inevitable fear of making a wrong decision.

In order to protect them from screwing up, their inner critic or sceptic will create a list of reasons not to buy. These are commonly called objections, fears and concerns. And within each industry or product class they're almost invariably the same.

So think about your business and your customers. Mentally step through your last few presentations and weed out the common denominators that customers raised as objections, fears, concerns or issues. What were they?

List them on a sheet of paper. Now drill into them a bit more and ask yourself if there were three recurring themes or common issues what would they be? You'll find that herein lies your acre of diamonds. A veritable hidden treasure. But you need to do something with them to access the real value.

First ask yourself, 'Can I do anything in advance of a customer raising these issues to allay their concerns?' If so, do it.

One of my top agents understands very well what people think about the bulk of the real estate industry. Not much! He knows that while he acts at all times with total integrity many others in the industry don't. As a result buyers and sellers often have a lot of cynicism, if not outright hostility, for agents.

So Matthew gives every potential client a list of his most recent clients with their phone numbers. (He always asks each client if he can add their name to his growing list prior to doing so.)

His explanation goes like this: 'Mr and Mrs Smith, one of the things I like to do for every new client is give them a list of all my previous clients. If there's anything you're concerned about with regard to appointing me to sell your home, feel free to call anyone on the list and check their experience with me.'

This strategy has helped him become one of the highest paid and most respected real estate people on the planet.

Why is it so effective? Firstly, Matthew is giving people an opportunity to independently verify everything he's told them. His credibility and their trust go up instantly. And secondly, he's helping his clients do their homework by providing easy-to-access references.

In short, Matthew is making it easier to choose him.

And you know what the most amazing thing is? People usually hire him without ever calling one reference, because they feel they can trust him as he's been so forthcoming.

14.

Marketing your business (and yourself)

The essence of marketing is meeting your customers' needs. It's not just about ads, brochures, websites or listings in the Yellow Pages. It's really about your attitude. It's about asking yourself, 'How can I serve my customers better today? How can I create world-class service? How can I convert my customers into raving fans of my business?'

You Inc. – marketing yourself

Not everyone reading this book will own their own business, or be a professional salesperson or senior manager. You might be unemployed, just starting on the first rung of the corporate ladder or working part time and nurturing secret entrepreneurial ambitions.

It doesn't matter what stage of your career you're at or what your official job title is, you can start building your marketing and business skills right now. All it takes is a new mindset. From now on, consider yourself as your own professional services company: You Inc. It doesn't matter whether you're a driveway attendant at a petrol station or you're a brand marketing manager, you're a business.

So ask yourself this question: would you buy shares in You Inc.? Do you see yourself worthy of being invested in? If not, you need to do something about that. How's your customer service? Every hour of every day provides multiple opportunities to provide great service. Every time you pick up the phone, it's a marketing exercise.

You might not think you have many customer interface opportunities. But everyone has internal and/or external customers. For example, say you're the Accounts Receivable Clerk. If you pick up the phone after 12 rings, don't introduce yourself and use a gruff tone, this reflects poorly on You Inc. However, if you pick up the phone on the second ring, with a smile and an introduction, use the caller's name, and are polite and pleasant, You Inc. is implementing excellent customer service standards.

Opportunities are created as a result. You're more likely to be noticed by your superiors and get a raise or a promotion. Other people might notice your great service as well. Perhaps a caller will say, 'I don't know what they're paying you over there, but you should come and work for us.'

So you need to work out what You Inc. needs to become a highly desirable investment. Work out a training program for your self-development. That could be to read six sales and customer service books a year, listen to inspirational tapes and go to self-development seminars.

Once you see yourself as a business, you'll start running yourself as a business. You need to have a budget, a cash flow forecast and an investment strategy. You need goals, a business plan and a marketing plan. You also need to start building up some assets.

Your net worth = your network

The most valuable asset of any business is your relationships. Without them you have nothing. You might not have anything to sell just yet, but that shouldn't stop you from building up a network of potential customers and useful contacts. Don't see them as someone else's customers. See them as relationships that you can build for your future business.

When I was starting out in real estate, I had a strategy for customer acquisition, even though I wasn't getting paid any commission. I just recognised early on that the relationships I was building were going to be the most valuable thing I had.

So start building a personal database to keep track of all the people you're dealing with. (It doesn't have to be fancy or high tech — even index cards will do.) Because every single day you have an opportunity to create another half a dozen relationships and build your net worth.

Be something to someone

One of the greatest mistakes I see many businesses making is trying to be all things to all people. Now their intention is extremely honourable — the desire to provide a great service or product to as many customers as possible. But the problem is this: in the pursuit of this ideal many miss the point, and that is...YOU CAN'T.

It's sad I know. But true. You must make a decision about who you are, what your area of specialness or uniqueness is, and how you can connect that with the most suitable audience.

Every individual on the planet is totally unique, but there are groups of people that enjoy, aspire to and gravitate towards the same things. These are called demographic segments. Some of the best known segments include Generation.com, Generation X, Baby Boomers, Single Career Females, Yuppies, Dinks and so on.

You can certainly work with a few of these segments simultaneously, but it's virtually impossible to create a product, service process, marketing model, image or sales team that will appeal to everyone across the board. So decide which segments you want to own. If you had to choose two, which would they be?

When I started selling houses I focused on young couples who were buying their first home. I was young myself and aspired to own my first home, so I could totally relate to where this group was at. I also saw that almost nobody else was servicing them because the sales at this end of the market didn't provide sales agents with the large commission cheques they wanted.

But it certainly worked for me, and I learned that servicing one segment extremely well paid handsome rewards.

Divide and conquer

An exception to this rule is an organisation that services multiple segments under different banners. For example, Toyota decided it wanted to get a slice of the luxury car market, yet were well and truly entrenched in the minds and hearts of car buyers as manufacturers of lower to middle priced cars.

So rather than confuse their core customers with a new range of high priced Toyotas, they decided to start a new brand called Lexus, which has been a remarkable success. Lexus is wholly owned by Toyota, but the entire brand, showrooms, sales teams and management group are totally separate.

We did the same thing at our company. We were a market leader in the $200,000 to $2 million range, but we wanted to attract business at the top end of the market. We realised that to evolve our brand to appeal to the upper market, we would risk losing some of our strong following at the lower end. So we decided to look around for another brand that we could grow alongside the McGrath brand. It could share the technology, infrastructure and intellectual capital we had developed, but would be run as a separate company exclusively selling properties above $3 million.

We looked around the market and considered the possibility of starting a new brand from scratch. But our feeling was that this end of the market was unlikely to embrace a start-up brand in the short term. The market we would be dealing with were high achievers, mature, established, international and somewhat risk averse when disposing of their most valuable asset.

After looking at all our options we decided the best direction was to approach Christie's Great Estates in the US. This group was an offshoot of the fine arts company and had arguably the world's greatest brand at the top end of the market, one of the most elite and exclusive customer bases and, most importantly for us, no representation in Australia.

I got on the phone to their head office and, as one might expect, found it challenging to gain their attention. Their business was growing rapidly in North America and just starting in Europe. Australia was certainly not a major part of their immediate plans.

However with persistence and sound reasoning (but mostly persistence) we were able to eventually get them interested in us flying the flag in Australia.

In less than two years of operation Christie's has become market leader in the lucrative luxury property market with over $300 million in sales last year.

There was no way in the world that our core brand could have achieved those results at the top end, and even if we had started heading in that direction it would have likely cost us elsewhere in lost sales.

Marketing is everything

Years ago I was talking to my close friend Siimon Reynolds, who is renowned as one of our country's best marketers. I took the opportunity to pick his brains, and I asked him what the best form of marketing was. What did he think that meant, was it any particular form of advertising or promotion, or was it logo or branding, or something else?

His reply was simple: marketing is everything you do. It's the brand of coffee you serve your customers, it's the music you play in reception, and it's how many rings the phone is answered on.

A lot of people think that marketing is all about glossy adverts, slick sales collateral and an impressive website. Of course all of these things are marketing, but marketing covers a whole lot more. It covers every interaction with the general public and all the ways you present yourself to the world.

When I was 20 years old I read a story about a Sam Walton who created the Wal-Mart retail empire in the US. He said, 'The best marketing I do is when the guy in parcel pick-up gently places a parcel in the back seat of a customer's car when they come down to collect it.' That philosophy had a huge impact on me. I was really impressed by the care he gave his customers and his understanding of the power of one-to-one marketing.

This is now the way we look at our business. We believe that every single thing we do is critical for building the brand, building relationships and building market share.

One-to-one marketing is an extremely powerful way to differentiate yourself from your competitors. In any market there are multiple brands offering very similar services, all backed by similar marketing programs. So the little things can make a big difference.

Take the real estate industry for example. There are many big franchises out there saying roughly the same thing with similar budgets. So how do you differentiate as a consumer? Well you can't until you walk into one of their offices and they give you a smile, sit you down and serve you a cappuccino. They have lovely fresh flowers and nice music, and someone greets you with a smile and listens to you and takes notes. That's all marketing.

A key marketing exercise for every business is to take a good look at every single thing that you do: every form and document you use, the presentation of your staff and premises, your phone manner, how you relate to customers... Take a look at every little thing and ask yourself if it could be improved to better serve your customers' needs.

Sometimes you're so familiar with your business that you miss the little things that could be improved. So get a pair of fresh eyes to come in and get someone who can be brutally honest. Because you've been walking past the same dusty silk flowers in reception for the last 10 years, you often don't see them anymore, but someone else will.

Do some focus groups with customers. Bring them in and ask them what it's like to do business with you. What do they like? What don't they like? For a principal, it's sometimes painful to listen to customers' feedback. Because if you chose the right customers — ones who can be totally honest — you're going to have to sit there for an hour or so with a knot in your stomach listening to how you screwed up.

But if you're committed to improving and growing the business the pain is worth it. Customer complaints are also a valuable form of feedback. Rather than dreading them, see complaints as a valuable source of information that can help you create a better customer experience.

An excellent source of ideas about how to improve your customer experience is other businesses. I've got my radar on 24/7 looking for great customer experiences and marketing ideas that I can incorporate in my business.

When I walk into the Ritz Carlton I immediately think, 'Why does this feel good?' So I look around, and there's someone polishing the brass plaque, and I say, 'Well that feels good to me. They've got someone polishing the plaque — they've got pride.' And then I wonder how we can incorporate that into the way we do business. Then I notice all the staff are wearing smart uniforms and are smiling, and I start thinking about the presentation of our staff, and so on.

So you see you don't have to be a fabulously creative marketer to create great marketing. I don't feel I've been particularly innovative with my business — I'm not creative at all. But I can have great customer experiences, and I notice what makes them special. I see what works — in lots of different markets and industries — and then assimilate these ideas into my business.

Getting the ideas is never a problem. You could sit on the Internet for an hour and you could get 100 great marketing ideas. The trick is actually taking action. You've got to take these ideas and you've got to implement them.

Innovation out of frustration: *Space* magazine

I was sitting at an open home inspection in 1985 and a customer came up to me and said (as a lot of customers did), 'Thanks John, but this property is not for me. What else have you got?' My reaction was to think about which of the properties I had listed was suitable for this buyer and write the address on a business card. I'd hand them the card and say, 'Why don't you have a look at this house?' Sometimes they'd check it out and sometimes they wouldn't.

I was frustrated with this because I felt it wasn't the most professional approach for dealing with clients. So I decided that in future I'd take brochures on every property I had listed to each open home inspection. I put together some brochures. They were just photocopies, but they had all the pertinent information and a floor plan and looked OK. So when someone asked what else I had I'd hand them three or four brochures.

Then my idea started to evolve. I thought, why don't I get all the brochures together, and if someone's not a buyer for this property, I'll hand them 20 brochures stapled together. Then I thought, why don't I put a cover on the front of it and add in some information about how to bid at auctions, what the stamp duty costs and other things that buyers want to know.

So I added in all this information and that was the beginning of *Space* magazine, which is now Australia's highest-quality property magazine. So what started out as just a bit of frustration about the standard of service I was offering slowly morphed into a fantastic marketing tool.

I continue to tweak it to this day. *Space* is not finished yet, its probably only 20% through its life cycle. Every week I look at it and I ask myself, 'How can we make this better? Is that a really compelling story? What advertisers do we want to get in here that will be relevant to our customers?'

Focus groups

Every quarter we get together with some of our customers and ask for their feedback about initiatives we've got in the pipeline. We say, 'We're thinking about doing this. What do you think?' They'll either say, 'It's a terrible idea – don't do it'. Or they'll say, 'That's a great idea', and inevitably they start spreading the word about it.

So it's a win-win situation. We get tremendous feedback and can create mini-evangelists for the business. Our customers get to share in our vision and feel good because we value their opinion, and they have a chance to get involved in our success.

Branding – your platform to greatness

A brand is built by combining a 'marketing is everything' mindset with your company values and mission. The brand is like the personality of the organisation. It's how you present yourself to, and interact with, the market.

Great brands immediately conjure up certain values and feelings in consumers' minds. If I say Apple you think of innovation. If I say IBM you think of dependability. If I say Ritz Carlton you think of high-quality service. You'll know you've got your branding right if the image and values you're trying to project are recognised immediately by every person who hears your name, sees your logo or ad, or walks by your office.

The brand is the platform upon which you will build your business to greatness. It's the platform upon which products and services are sold, your advertising is developed, your sales collateral is created, your corporate image is designed and your office is decorated.

It's also the platform from which you recruit staff. We know that we get a better response to our employment ads if we put a McGrath logo on them than if we advertise through an outside recruitment agency. It's because people relate to our brand. They know what we stand for and people want to be a part of that.

You should tackle the issue of brand early in the development of your business and revisit it regularly. Ask yourself what you want your brand to stand for. I probably spend 25% of my time on our brand, either in meetings talking about the brand, thinking about the brand or working on evolving it with the marketing team. Our management team is constantly discussing the brand. Is it still exactly the same, is it changing, what is it now, what should it be?

So every time I give a speech, I have some clarity around how we want to represent McGrath. Every time we redesign an office we consider which of our values we would like to project. Are we going for innovation, are we going for trust, are we going for openness?

We've built the McGrath brand up over a period of time. We've been able to develop it through PR and advertising, through editorial, through consistency of look and feel, through comments made in the press, through speeches that we've given, through seminars we've held and most of all by being customer-focused and creating raving fans. The essence of our brand infuses everything we do.

Every single thing we do is critical to maintaining the integrity of the brand. We can have *Space* magazine, we can have nice offices and we can have a cool website, but I gotta tell you, if someone turns up at an open home inspection, if the agent is one minute late, if they're not helpful, if they're not organised, if they're not focused, if they don't use the customer's name — then our brand has just flown out the window.

So consistency is absolutely crucial. I know if I do a seminar, it's got to be fantastic. So if my team say, 'Well we can get the cheap instant coffee,' I'll say, 'No, we've got to get the best coffee and we've got to get a barista to make it properly.' They might say that's going to cost another $200. Well that's cheap if it's going to build the brand.

Building a solid brand also provides you with a platform to move your business in new directions. I heard that Gerry Harvey plans to open a chain of boutique stores selling small electrical items. I thought to myself, Harvey Norman sells the same products as a number of other electrical appliance stores, but they've done an extraordinary job of building their brand.

So when they roll out a new venture they can leverage the huge amounts of brand recognition and customer familiarity and trust they've built up. As a result they have a much greater chance of success than someone launching a new brand does.

Triple bottom line

In the business world today, there's a wonderful sea change happening. CEOs, boards of directors, shareholders and employees are all starting to understand there's a much bigger picture in the corporate world than just making money. People are saying, 'Hey, that's a great company, not just because they have a big profit, but because they grow their people, they support their community, they take care of the environment and they're a good corporate citizen.'

The community is now very aware of these issues and demands responsible corporate citizenship. I believe companies that are creating profits without conscience are going to become dinosaurs. In our business we report to the Board of Directors, not only on our profit, but also on our contribution to the community and how we're helping to protect the environment.

I encourage businesspeople to start thinking not only about their sales, marketing and profit results, but also how much they have contributed. How would your contribution balance look at the end of the year? I'm not just talking about financial contributions either. You could offer your services as a business mentor or speaker, help out at the school fete or give a lecture to the year five kids about leadership. Or you could make a commitment to using as many recyclable supplies as possible.

World-class customer service

When was the last time you experienced world-class customer service?

I bet that's got you scratching your head. Not too many people can answer that question without racking their memory. We're bombarded with so many service experiences every day, and yet so few of them ever stand out.

With improvements in manufacturing and quality control there are now only very little differences in quality between products in the same class. There's not much between a Holden Commodore and a Ford Falcon these days. So product marketers are increasingly relying on service as a way of differentiating their offerings.

And in the service industries, their service is their product, so to stay ahead of their competitors they've had to lift their game as well. Customer service standards have been raised across the board, and so have customers' expectations. People are a lot more discerning and expect good service from everyone they do business with.

I often say to my team, 'You know guys, we're being judged against the Ritz Carlton, not against LJ Hooker down the road.' My point is that people are experiencing great service from many different businesses in many different industries. And these experiences set their expectations for good service across the board. So when someone receives fabulous customer service at the Ritz Carlton, that becomes the benchmark against which they will judge you.

So good service is now the entry point for all businesses. The entry level is meeting people's expectations. If you can't do that, you're history. And if you want to really prosper you've got to do much better than that. You've got to offer world-class customer service.

Without love, it's just coffee

Service is the ultimate differentiator. Having a great product or service is important. But don't kid yourself that that's enough these days. In a rapidly developing global marketplace, whatever your product (or service) is, someone can probably make it as well or better than you if they try hard enough. The big difference is how it's served.

There is a chain of coffee shops in the US called Café Espresso. At one of their AGMs the CEO, Jeff Taylor, was talking about what their company actually does. He explained that every day there are thousands of people making drinks from ground coffee beans and hot water, putting them in china cups, setting them down on tables and counters, and charging $2.50. But the difference between them and us, he went on, is that Café Espresso does it with love. 'Without love, it's just coffee,' he said.

You can imagine the different customer experiences of being served a cup of coffee versus being served a cup of coffee with love. Which one would you prefer? So you can see how powerful a customer service focus can be.

What is world-class customer service?

World-class customer service is significantly exceeding a customer's expectations. We call them 'service wows'. That's service that's so good and so unexpected it becomes a topic of dinner party conversation. I'll give you a few examples:

One of the things I did when people moved into a house I'd just sold them, was give them the services of a handyman for a day. A few days after they'd moved in, I'd send them a little note saying I'd hired a handyman for a day's work as a gift from me to them. I'd include a list of the things the handyman could do, such as hanging paintings, putting up shower screens or oiling a sticky hinge, and give them his contact number so they could arrange for him to visit at a convenient time.

I also did a great deal with a pizza place. I said to them, 'If I could introduce you to a new local customer or two every week, would it be worth your while investing in one or two free pizzas?' So we did a deal where he gave me vouchers for free pizzas and I passed them on to people who'd just moved into a house I'd sold. I sent a note with the voucher saying, 'Welcome to Paddington. Here's a voucher for a free pizza. You're probably tired from moving and haven't unpacked your pots and pans yet, so why don't you call up and get a pizza delivered. It's on us.'

So when I was providing great service, my motivation was partly selfish. I was doing it for me as well as for my customers. I used to love the reaction I'd get from people and I used to love the feeling I got when I knew I'd done a great job.

So businesses that provide only mediocre service are not only letting down their customers, they're cheating themselves.

Charlie Trotter's – the WOW! factor

I used to go to the US quite regularly to share ideas with other top real estate agents. One time we were meeting in Chicago and the organiser of the meeting, my friend and mentor Bob Bohlen, announced he had a surprise treat for us. He was taking everyone to Charlie Trotter's for dinner.

My American colleagues had been raving about Charlie Trotter's for months. It's one of the best restaurants in the world, with a string of international awards and rave reviews. It's so popular you have to book three months in advance to get a table on the weekend. As I expected from its reputation, the food and service were outstanding. It was the best meal I ever had.

What also really impressed me was their business formula. Not only was Charlie Trotter a culinary genius, but he'd implemented some innovative operating procedures. He had married the creative with the operational to create a hugely successful restaurant.

The restaurant industry is notoriously fickle with a high mortality rate. There are lots of variables which are difficult to control. How many customers will book this week? How many walk-ins will we have? When will everyone want to eat? How much food do we need to order? Wastage, in both food and labour, can be crippling.

So Trotter created a formula to give himself some clarity and control in these areas. At his restaurant you must book a table and there are two sittings each night, one at 6 p.m. and one at 9 p.m. Instead of an à la carte menu you have a choice of three set dégustation menus. They have a set price and you make your choice when you book.

The result is that Trotter goes to the market each day and knows exactly how many customers he has tonight, what they're going to eat and how much money he has to spend on produce. Instead of leaving himself to the mercy of the variables, he took control.

But the real stroke of genius came the next day when Bob Bohlen got a phone call from Trotter's maître d'. I was in Bob's car at the time and he put the call on speakerphone. 'I just wanted to check that your meal last night was up to your satisfaction and expectation,' the maître d' said. 'Did your guests enjoy the meal? If you'd like to visit us again please give me a call.'

I was blown away. I mean how many times has a restaurant rung you back and asked how your meal was? The answer is probably none. That phone call added the WOW! factor. It completely exceeded my expectations and turned me into a raving fan. I've told this story in my seminars and sung Charlie Trotter's praises to literally tens of thousands of people.

So ask yourself, what's going to be your 'Charlie Trotter phone call' that turns your customers into raving fans?

Moments of truth

Your most valuable asset is delighted customers. Every time you interact with a customer you have an opportunity to improve this asset. So it's really important to focus on your customer touch points, which Jan Carlzon called the 'moments of truth' in his book of the same name. Carlzon was head of the Scandinavian Air System (SAS) in the 1980s. The airline was losing money when he took over and it was his responsibility to improve things.

He calculated that in one year, each of SAS's 10 million customers came in contact with approximately five SAS staff. So they had 50 million opportunities to prove to their customers that SAS was the best airline. Carlzon strongly believed these moments of truth would ultimately determine whether SAS would succeed or fail as a company.

So he put a series of service standards in place so that at every moment of truth the customer would be delighted. When someone was checking in for a flight, instead of the check-in attendant just gruffly stamping their ticket and throwing their bag on the conveyor, the attendant would look them in the eye and say, 'Welcome Miss James. Thanks for flying SAS today.' They'd pick up your bag and gently place it on the conveyor belt and say, 'I hope you enjoy your flight.'

The airline's moments of truth went from 'let's get these passengers moving' to 'let's take 15 seconds to delight this passenger'. It had an enormously positive effect. SAS returned to high profitability and was awarded airline of the year.

Maintaining standards

Once you've recognised what your moments of truth are, and put some service standards in place for them, the next step is to instigate a monitoring process to make sure you stay on track.

We now send out an e-survey to everyone we do business with within minutes of them transacting. So if someone exchanges a property at 9.00 a.m., the email is automatically sent, arriving in their email inbox shortly thereafter.

We ask 10 questions relating to the service experience, and the customer rates us from zero to 10. It takes about one minute to complete. We are now getting daily feedback on customers' experiences, because it's such an important area for us.

We also have mystery buyers going around to our *open for inspections*, ringing up our offices and visiting our offices in person. They report back to us on what the experience was like, how it felt, were they looked after, did our staff seem to care, did they follow up, did they call you by name? We also have quarterly focus groups where we get six to eight buyers in a room. We say, 'Hey, all you guys just bought last month, tell us truthfully what it was like. What was really good? Where did we screw up? Did you deal with another agent during your purchase that was doing something better than us? Tell us about that.'

Word of mouth – build your business one customer at a time

How do you build a great business? One customer at a time. How do you create a customer? One experience at a time. Make sure that when someone walks in your door they receive the best possible service you can provide. When they leave they'll feel good about dealing with you and they'll be back. Plus, they'll tell their friends. And then your business just grows and grows.

With the Internet and mobile communications there's more ways than ever to market your business. But the most powerful form of marketing is still word of mouth. Without a doubt. Forget the fact that Sony will probably spend hundreds of millions this year on marketing. The best way to build any business is by word of mouth marketing and referral.

Sometimes I say to one of our agents, 'You're with a homebuyer, you've qualified them and made your presentation. What's the outcome you're after?' 9 out of 10 will say: 'Sell the house.' That's what nearly everyone in the real estate industry would say.

My preferred outcome is to sell 50 properties with the customer. I want them to have such a great experience selling their house with me that they tell their family, friends and co-workers. I want to be not only their agent of choice, but also the agent they refer to anyone they meet who is selling their house. I want to do business with everyone in their sphere of influence.

And you'd agree there's a big difference in the way you treat someone if they represent only one sale, compared to someone who potentially may bring 50 sales. You naturally have a much higher level of attentiveness, customer service and passion to make sure you deliver in this moment.

The question I asked myself was, 'What's the lifetime opportunity of every customer's interaction?' Focus on that and then treat every customer based on their lifetime opportunity, not just as one potential sale.

Someone walks into your clothing shop. You can either look at them and say, 'They're probably not going to buy anything. Maybe they'll buy one dress from me.' Or you can say, 'This person could refer 150 clients to me.'

So you look after them, give them a beautiful cappuccino and sit them down and give them great service and advice. Don't try and sell them something that's not right for them. You might follow them up by dropping by their office tomorrow with a new sample that you think they'll like. It's so easy to build your business when you've got that mindset of 'a customer for life'.

Rarely do you end up coming across a customer that is a one-time transaction, if you get it right, they're 50 to 100 transactions down the track.

Create raving fans

Simply stated, a customer is someone that does business with you. Obviously every business needs customers to survive. But to be really successful you need more than customers. You need raving fans. A raving fan is someone who does business with you and has such a great experience they're just bursting to tell everyone they see how good it was.

How do you turn your customers into raving fans? Simple: you over-deliver on their expectations. Constantly ask yourself, 'How can I improve the quality of our customer experience? How can I make our customers feel special?' Always remember that the reason you're in business is to serve that person that walks in your door called the customer.

Dealing with unhappy customers

In spite of all your best intentions, sometimes you don't meet your customers' expectations and they can get upset. You have to accept unhappy customers as a fact of life. Many businesspeople dread this situation and consequently they freak out and avoid dealing with the issue, which can be very detrimental to the business.

A dissatisfied customer is both a threat and an opportunity. The threat is they'll start bad-mouthing you around town and undermine all the effort you've put into creating world-class service and building your brand. The opportunity is that by dealing with the customer's complaint promptly and effectively you can build a much stronger relationship with them and even turn them into a raving fan. In fact, it might even be easier to turn a dissatisfied customer into a raving fan.

From problems to raving fans

I heard about a study in the US where a software developer deliberately put a small bug in the latest version of their product. They sent the buggy software to a small number of customers, with the rest receiving the fully functioning product.

Some time later they did a customer service survey. The customers who had received the good software were happy with the service they'd received — it was OK. But the customers who'd received the bad software were much more positive about the service they'd received. They said, 'It was fantastic, we had a couple of little hitches early on, but the technicians were great. They came out immediately and fixed the problem, and they were very pleasant and easy to deal with.'

So the next time a customer has a complaint or problem, don't avoid the issue, but take the opportunity to create a raving fan.

Because when you deal with a customer's problem you can create a much stronger relationship with them than if they never had a problem in the first place.

Deal with complaints fast

When you have a complaint from a customer it's imperative that you deal with it immediately. If you have a message that says one of your customers is unhappy, that's the call you have to return first. Because as every minute passes with the issue unresolved, the customer's anger and dissatisfaction grows. The likelihood that they'll start telling their friends and colleagues about their displeasure increases. So get straight onto them.

Neutralise the ill feeling

Sometimes you upset a customer and despite your best efforts you can't turn them into a raving fan. However, you can almost always neutralise any ill feeling. We've had situations where a buyer has their heart set on a property, and just at the last minute another buyer comes out of the woodwork and puts a bigger cheque on the table and buys it. Sometimes the unsuccessful buyer blames us.

We can't always turn them around and have them love us, but what we can do is take the anger out of how they might feel. We do that through listening to their complaint, and making an effort to understand how they feel. We don't use gimmicky gifts or self-serving excuses, but we deal with their issue in a genuine manner and make a humble apology.

Dealing with customer complaints in eight steps

I believe that dealing with customer complaints is such an important part of our customer service that I have developed an eight-step process for dealing with them. I've had the eight steps printed on laminated cards and every member of our team has one in their desk. The eight steps are as follows:

1. Give your total attention

Drop everything and focus all your attention on the customer. Don't be on the phone and writing an email at the same time, saying, 'Yes, what was your problem?' when the customer can hear you typing in the background.

2. Be calm and patient

Recognise that someone who makes a complaint is going to be emotionally charged. They may be feeling angry and/or upset. So you've got to be calm so as not to make them more agitated, and give them all the time they need.

3. Listen – don't interrupt

When someone makes a complaint, what they want more than anything is to get it off their chest. To be heard. So just listen and let them tell their story.

4. 'I understand how you feel'

As well as wanting to tell their story, the customer wants you to understand how they feel. They don't want you to give them excuses or defend your position. They want you to relate to them and say, 'I really understand how you feel, and if I was in your shoes, I'd be just as upset as you are.'

5. Get all the information

In order to rectify the complaint you must get all the details. Note down the who, what, where, when and why of their problem.

6. Apologise and say 'Thank you'

Not only should you tell the customer you're sorry they feel this way, you should thank them for bringing this complaint to your attention. 'Look I'm really sorry about this Stephen. I want to thank you for bringing it to my attention. It's important for us to know when things don't go right so we can improve our service.'

7. Commit to take responsibility

You must take full responsibility for the problem and let your customer know that. Even if you delegate fixing the problem you should report back to the customer yourself.

8. Advise next steps and timing, and follow through

Let the customer know straightaway how you intend to handle the problem and when they can expect to hear back from you.

15.

Does change last?

Now we've come to the end of the book I hope you're fired up with loads of ideas and inspiration to help you create a great business and a great life. But perhaps you've got some nagging doubts about whether it's possible for you to create the life you've dreamed of.

Perhaps you made some changes in the past, but they haven't been lasting. You started out with the best intentions, but somewhere along the way you lost motivation and you drifted back to your old ways.

What you must realise is that motivation doesn't last. But, hey, neither does taking a shower! Every morning you jump in the shower and get squeaky clean. But by the end of the day you need another shower, and the next morning you have another shower.

You don't wake up in the morning and think, 'Don't tell me I have to take another shower today.' You just do it because it's become a part of your routine. So just as you take daily showers, you must get into the habit of giving yourself regular motivation.

Keep your goals up to date and go over them regularly. Surround yourself with inspiring people, read books and attend seminars. Make a commitment to improve every day and give yourself rewards for doing so. Make sure you take regular exercise and eat healthy foods.

When you start making changes in your life it can be hard to overcome the inertia at first. But once you get started you'll soon start to see small improvements that inspire you to keep going. You learn how to maximise your outcomes and minimise your effort and you begin to enjoy the process even more.

From my own experience and by investigating the success of others, I know that lasting change is possible. If the change is significant and fast enough, and it feels good, it will become the new you. The key is to stay motivated.

If you're committed, they're minor inconveniences

There are always going to be challenges, difficulties and setbacks in your life. Things don't always go as well as you might like. For some people these setbacks might be disasters which stop them reaching their goals. For others they're just minor inconveniences. It all comes down to your mindset.

Just accept that every single day on your journey to greatness there are going to be many divots in the road and boulders you've got to go around. It's all part of the process. If you're committed, you'll just find a way around them and keep moving towards your goals. After a while you don't even notice them anymore.

The door will open

Achieving success is a little bit like the sliding doors at airports. You walk towards the closed doors and at first nothing happens.

You take a few more steps. Still closed, but you keep going anyway. Just at the last moment as you approach, they whoosh open and you're on your way.

To open the doors of success you've got to keep moving towards them — even when you fear they might not open. You've got to have clarity about what you want to achieve. You've got to have confidence and faith that if you keep moving in that direction and stay true to your goals and commitments, the door will open. You've just got to keep going.

Good luck.

The Most Valuable Lesson I Have Learned:
Over 100 Success Concepts to Change your Life

John McGrath

THE MOST
VALUABLE
LESS●NS
I HAVE
LEARNED

Over 100 Success Concepts
to Change your life

John McGrath

To create something great, first you must have the vision.

Then take action.

With a strategy of combining many small wins day in day out, John McGrath shares the concepts that have helped inspire him to achieve his goals.

The Most Valuable Lessons I Have Learned will help you realise the power to keep your attitude positive and your energy strong.

ISBN: 0732276373

YOU DON'T HAVE TO BE B RN BRILLIANT

How to Design
a Magnificent Life

John McGrath

You Don't Have to Be Born Brilliant:
How to Design a Magnificent Life

John McGrath

Why is it that a handful of the population achieve phenomenal results and the majority struggle to keep their heads above water?

Same circumstances, same period of time and same sorts of opportunities, yet radically different results.

How to Design a Magnificent Life

Real success is something that eludes most of us, but it doesn't have to.

In a world so full of opportunities it is within everyone's power to turn their life around. Whether in our career, relationships, health or finances, John McGrath believes we are all capable of seizing opportunities and turning failure into advantage if we change our attitude - attitude is everything.

Success is just as much about 'unlearning' as it is about 'learning': about losing the habits that have been holding you back and replacing them with strategies, attitudes and actions that will take you to new levels of achievement.

YOU DON'T HAVE TO BE BORN BRILLIANT is about achieving magnificence in every area of your life.

ISBN: 0733607969

Also available in audio